EARTH MEMORIES

Llewelyn Powys

EARTH MEMORIES

REDCLIFFE
Bristol

First published in 1934
by John Lane The Bodley Head Ltd.

This edition first published
in 1983 by Redcliffe Press Ltd,
14 Dowry Square, Bristol 8

ISBN 0 905459 43 1

Photoset and printed in Great Britain by
Photobooks (Bristol) Ltd,
Barton Manor, St. Philips, Bristol BS2 0RN

CONTENTS

CONTENTS

INTRODUCTION

"I think Llewelyn," wrote Somerset Maugham of the Powys brothers, "by living so long cheek by jowl with death, alone of them learnt to be honest." The comment was no doubt meant to be provocative, in the Thirties. But in a way it still is. For although we know Theodore Francis Powys, one of the few contemporary writers to be approved by *Scrutiny*, and John Cowper Powys, if "know" is the word to use of that gigantic mythopoeic literary volcano whose works are still in process of assimilation by an industrious ant-army of critics, are we any nearer knowing Llewelyn?

And yet, of the three, Llewelyn is the easiest to know. To open nearly any of his books is to find him talking, in an extraordinary blend of modern English with Urquhart and Thomas Deloney, about his own life and convictions, his childhood at Montacute Vicarage in Somerset, his idle undergraduate days at Cambridge, his time as a farm manager in Africa and a freelance writer in America. Talking, moreover, not with the insistence of egotism, but as a way of sharing and celebrating experience with oddly-precise epithets and an occasional streak of rueful self-caricature, until suddenly his attention turns to man's predicament, to love and death; the whole architecture of the page changes, and the long sentences go sweeping on, clause after clause, at once impersonal and the apotheosis of personality, the embodiment of meaning rather than the assertion of it, the rhetoric that is Llewelyn Powys and nobody else.

1

To know Llewelyn is, inevitably, to know the other Powyses. The eighth of six sons and five daughters born to the Reverend Charles Francis Powys between 1872 and 1890, he was always passionately close to his family, and the devotion was returned: "without doubt," according to John Cowper Powys, "Llewelyn was the best loved *of* all his brothers and sisters *by* all his brothers and sisters". "We're Powyses, you and me, Powyses, *Powyses*, don't you see?" was how a friend summarised the almost comic intensity of their family feeling. Time and again he describes the late Victorian life at the vicarage, the lamps, the long walks, the tennis parties, the elder sons reading the lesson in church. Theodore, in later life, would speak of "your father" and "your brother"; Llewelyn never sought to distance himself in this way from those he loved and the happy life they had shared.

To some extent he was influenced by them. He followed his brothers to Cambridge, where he did not distinguish himself, taking a pass degree. He spent the World War years in Africa with his brother Willie; after the war, he went to America, where John Cowper was earning a precarious and exhausting living as a lecturer. Llewelyn abandoned lecturing after one attempt—lacking John's histrionic power, he was an embarrassing failure—but remained there for several years, "writing for the papers" as he deprecatingly called it, for the example of John and Theodore was always before him. Returning home, he finally found Theodore's way of living suited him best: with Alyse Gregory, his American wife, he settled in a remote cottage in Dorset, writing ever more deeply of his own memories and convictions. All these experiences were valuable to him, remote from his character though some of them seem in retrospect. His books about Africa, *Ebony and Ivory* and *Black Laughter*, gained him an accidental reputation in America as a sort of Conrad or R. B. Cunningham Graham. John Cowper has said that Llewelyn was famous in America, and Theodore in England, long before anyone had heard of him.

In one way, Llewelyn was a natural writer. His letters are vivid and personal, and often very funny. His first published work, part of *Confessions of Two Brothers* (1916) written with John Cowper, showed how easily he could dramatise his own experience, a talent he came to recognise as his principal gift (the family called it "Lulu-ising"). Yet in another he found writing desperately hard. A remark by Theodore that "there was always something wrong about writers who could not write about anything but themselves" depressed him deeply. Although he wrote one highly readable novel, *Apples Be Ripe* (1930), he could not think of plots. Literary journalism, in which "new subjects" were all-important, was a strain for him.

What set Llewelyn apart from his brothers, and indeed shaped his whole life, was ill health. The first essay in this collection describes the onset of tuberculosis when he was twenty-five, and its subsequent visitations, and makes clear the extent to which it shocked him. For he had never been a weakling: as an American friend said, there was "nothing of the invalid in his looks or manner". Tall, with tightly-curled sandy-gold hair, he seemed to link his own exuberance to the native Powys toughness, nor for all his Epicurean convictions was he given to any sort of damaging excess. "Not Lulu, not Lulu ill," cried John Cowper when he heard. It was a kind of outrage.

The existing elements of his character were immediately and permanently polarised. No writer has been more constantly aware of the fact of death, of extinction, of joining "that recumbent congregation of all nationalities that lie upon their shoulder-blades". He could never forget that

> it was I, and I alone, who, when all my dramatisations and sensationalisms were over, would be spending cold nights, cold years, cold centuries, alone in a cold elmwood coffin.

It became the central plank of his philosophy. Who, with this certainty before him, could be concerned with social observance and advancement? Or regard religion's preposterous bait of immortality with anything but angry contempt? Or help striving daily, as he wrote to an American enquirer in 1932, "to grow accustomed to the prospect of death with a serene mind"?

Yet it was not a negative reaction. The overwhelming importance of death was balanced by the overwhelming importance of living: "love every moment of life," he wrote on his death-bed, "that you experience *without pain*."

> Consider the glow, the glory of being alive, the incredible chance of it! How heart-piercing, how shocking, how supremely beautiful is this unexplained, wavering movement that troubles all that is, from the Milky Way to a common sting-nettle!

Endless variations on this theme can be found in books such as *Now That The Gods are Dead* and *Glory of Life*; in the present collection, the essays *Natural Happiness* and *Natural Worship* take it up again. At first sight his prose looks unfashionably "grand", not entirely free of what he himself called "flagrant clichés" and "bloody banalities", together with the affectation of neo-Jacobethanisms such as "both maid and yellow-hosed bachelor". What saves it is his vehement and idiosyncratic vision; only he could write of

4

slugs that "with silent secret perspicacity, draw towards the undefended seedlings of their appetites", or

> Men and women, these bounding apes that must every day void dross, by a sweepstake chance have won divine thought, thought potent to destroy, potent to save.

The chief glory of life, inevitably, was sexual love and sexual enjoyment. "It is the backbone of all life, the pliable, beautiful, spiked backbone upon which the fair grace of the flesh is built."

> Lust is nature's free gift to us all, and the hours of its consummation are beyond all measure the most real and ecstatic hours of our lives.

After the mid-century revolution of our attitudes, such declarations may sound quaintly over-emphatic, but this is because they have been embraced rather than repudiated. Nor were they the hectic fancies of one deprived by upbringing and illness of direct sexual experience. The remarkable letters from Llewelyn to a young American poetess Gamel Woolsey, edited in 1973 by Malcolm Elwin as a footnote to his admirable biography, demonstrate that, where love was concerned, he spoke as he found. And so we are led to his last major book, the "imaginary auto-biography" *Love and Death* that arose from this strange relationship, in which the dying narrator recalls his passionate love for a girl who ultimately deserted him, reliving each episode to keep the thought of death at arm's length. In it Llewelyn's two great preoccupations are brought face to face, and the result is an audacious and poignant narrative richly summarising the desperate joyful brevity of life as he had known it.

In his later years of illness he grew a beard: the impulsive gold-haired young man with the "woman's mouth" became a gaunt figure in a cloak and broad-brimmed hat, something of a sage. "I'd forgotten how *wise* he became," a friend said, reading his letters after his death, and it is true that Llewelyn Powys is one of the rare writers who teach endurance of life as well as its enjoyment. To love life and grow accustomed to the prospect of death is a simple enough message, yet in fulfilling it he learnt not only to be honest, as Maugham said, but to distil into literature the example of his own sensibility and courage.

For at the end of all—what are we? A herd of dream cattle, images of breath, passing shadows that move swiftly across the world's pastures to a graveyard where, at a single clap, eternity is as a day and a day as eternity.

A STRUGGLE FOR LIFE

IT was in the month of November of the year 1909 that I first discovered I was suffering from pulmonary tuberculosis. Up till that time, although I had been conscious of feeling unwell, I had never suspected the serious nature of my malady. Probably it was fortunate that the disease so early in its advance broke a blood vessel. I was immediately examined by a doctor, who declared that I must leave England for a health-resort in Switzerland as soon as ever I was in a fit state to travel. Meanwhile the windows of my bedroom were removed from their frames and for three weeks I lay on my back contemplating the bare elms and misty autumnal roof-tops of the town of Sherborne, from, as it were, some open barn-loft unprotected from the weather.

Always of a nervous temperament, the doctor's diagnosis had been no small shock. As each morning I was waked from my restless dreams by the ringing of the bell of the convent in Long Street it seemed incredible that it was I, already so inordinate a lover of life, who had been selected as a victim to this terrible disease, selected almost certainly to die young.

I feel ashamed now when I think of how I dramatised my illness, talking incessantly of what it felt like to be dying, to be dying of consumption! My five brothers came to my bedside and with each of them in turn I discussed my fate. And as the rain drifted gustily in on to the bare deal floor, which in consequence gave out continually the curious chilled smell of a room where scrubbing has lately been in

7

progress, they would lend their attention to the subject with philosophic detachment, treating it in a tone as frank as my own, for all the world like five disillusioned jackdaws gathering about one of their kind who has been winged by a sportsman's gun. I asserted emphatically that if I lived to be thirty I should be satisfied.

The excitement of going to Switzerland kept me in good spirits; though occasionally it happened, in spite of all my bravado, that I became conscious of a dull uneasy sense of lonely apprehension as though I were about to set out upon a journey the length and weariness of which I could not foresee. For example, when a workman from the village at home who had come to visit me casually remarked that I had a "churchyard cough" I felt myself immediately wide awake to the reality of my predicament, a predicament devoid of sentiment, bereft of drama, bleak, unpretentious, and *natural*.

The first few months of my stay in Switzerland saw me recovering rapidly. If I had had the wit to return to England then, all might have been well; instead I allowed myself to be persuaded to stay on through the summer so as "to make sure of my cure." Immediately I became careless and spent time diverting myself in the company of patients who were sick in bed. I believe by this means I reinfected myself, for otherwise I can in no way account for the fact that my sickness, quite unexpectedly, took a turn for the worse. The disease now advanced more rapidly than it had ever done. All the dreaded symptoms of consumption began to show themselves. I felt poisoned, listless, and would easily fall asleep only to wake up drenched with sweat. Each night my cheeks burned with an ever-increasing fever. Each time that I was weighed it was found that I had lost several pounds. In a few weeks I became so thin that I could easily enclose my thigh in the small circle made by holding my two thumbs and two first fingers together. My decline had been so rapid that it seemed certain I should be dead within a few months. I could tell by their discreet manners that the Sanatorium doctors thought as much. Every time I coughed, with a sickening sense of impending physical disaster, I tasted corruption, as though at its very centre my body harboured some foul mildew.

My attitude to mortality has always been childish. Invariably when I contemplate death my thoughts turn to the fate of my body, as though my timorous consciousness would still be aware of what happens to it after I am dead. Looking now into the future I shivered, my mind recoiling desperately from the thought that before the Christmas of 1910 I would be a member of that recumbent congregation of all nationalities who lie on their shoulder-blades, under the mountain snow, row upon row of them, to the right and to the left of the black-spired Protestant church of Davos-Platz.

Then on the night of July 11th I had a haemorrhage. The shock of it caused me to tremble from crown to heel; but I believe, for all that, it saved my life, clearing away much diseased tissue and allowing me, as it were, to make a fresh start in my struggle for life. In the early part of the night the doctors were at my bedside constantly injecting me with gelatine. Later, they were called away to a neighbouring room to attend a young English boy named Burton who also had been taken suddenly ill. All through that night my abrupt fits of coughing, the particular significance of which could not be mistaken by anyone acquainted with the sickness, were answered by the abrupt fits of coughing of my friend, as he also gasped for breath, in his small hygienic room on the further side of the white corridor. Towards

9

morning the blood ceased to flow and I lay on my back not daring to move, watching a moth crawl up and down the flat impassive face of a large window-pane which already had received upon its surface the first pale indications of dawn. After the haemorrhage I remained in bed for four months. Throughout this time I was under the care of a Norwegian nurse to whose tireless devotion I have always felt I owe my life. Three weeks after the attack I was allowed to see my friend Wilbraham. I asked for news of Burton. "Burton! Why, Burton has been dead and buried—three weeks ago."

Slowly, very slowly, my temperature came down. For months I lay quite still looking out at the broken edge of a mountain-top on the other side of the Frauenkirk Valley. I looked at it in the morning when it was bleak and hard, I looked at it in the evening when, long after the setting sun had left the white roof of the hospital in which I was, its lofty clefts held fanciful rose-red shadows. The bare outline of this particular mountain suggested the exact shape of a woman lying on her back—her nose, her breasts, her knees, her toes even, limned against infinity. "Queen Victoria 'curing'," the more vulgar English patients called her.

I can well remember when I first, with the support of a serving-man, tried to get out of bed only to find my legs give under me like bent straws. The fact that my temperature was coming down filled me now with renewed hope. Slowly I grew better. I managed to get downstairs for the Christmas dinner. Each small advance filled me with exultation. So nervous was I, lest I should have another haemorrhage, that for months whenever I was dressed and moving about I would unconsciously be pressing my fingers against the right side of my chest, in an absurd endeavour to hold my damaged lung together as one might some precious fragile vessel. I wore a circular hole in a good serge waistcoat by this trick. An X-ray examination revealed that both my lungs were affected, but the right lung more seriously than the left.

By the end of January I began once more to take walks out of doors. At first a distance of a hundred yards would be sufficient to send my temperature up, but I soon discovered that such exercise-fever would come down as a rule after half an hour's rest on my *lieger* chair. This encouraged me to lengthen my walks, each day going a little further, but keeping all the time a careful watch on my temperature, which after rest would drop to normal. If it did not drop, then I concluded I had done too much and would in consequence reduce the length of my walks. Following this method I went first as far as the Kurhaus, then as far as the cattle shed where the crisp frosty air would be so pleasantly tainted; then, eventually, by the end of March, as far as the old white mill which stands by the river where the road winds its way down to the Frauenkirk village. Indeed, so proud was I of this last achievement that I marked one of its walls with my pocket knife.

It was now decided that I should return to England. My brother John came to fetch me. I well remember how impressed he was by the spectacle of the Davos "main street," every balcony of every house filled with prostrate human figures. An English clergyman passed us on his way to the skating rink. "Aye!" my brother exclaimed. "How one would like to see Our Lord come round that corner where the sleigh stands, with the twelve following behind Him disputing among themselves over some nice theological point."

We landed in England on May Day. I was overjoyed to be back again. After the snow-clad mountain landscape of the Engadine the fresh green of the Somerset meadows seemed wonderful. I found myself as sensitive to the sights and sounds and smells of the countryside as a brown hare in a field of sprouting corn. I remember one day meeting Fred Chant, the woodcutter, as I came out of the little back lane where the poplars grew and where Will Hockey's old grey mare used to graze. "They doctors can mend ye, Master Llewelyn," he said, "but they cannot cure ye; patch ye up for the summer, maybe, but you'll soon *be wearing a green coat* for all thick there syrup ye sip." The wearing of a green coat I knew referred to the grass of the churchyard which, so he anticipated, would soon be covering my bones.

It was not to be. To the astonishment of everybody my walks continued to lengthen, until I came to regard it as absolutely necessary for my health to walk at least ten miles each day, no less a distance being sufficient, so I considered, to bring about the required reactions. During that summer I came to know every lane and bypath around Montacute; the character of each field gate, whether it was stiff or easy to open; the places where there were gaps in the hedges; and the places where the banks of the deep muddy Somerset streams fell away so as to allow of a drinking-pool for the cattle. Under this combination of steady exercise and periods of complete rest my physical condition became extremely robust. It seemed that in a short time I would be quite well again.

The autumns in South Somerset are always damp. The woods at that time of the year give out the cloying smell of those small yellow toadstools that grow at the foot of decaying trees. My brother, T. F. Powys, realising this asked me to stay with him in Dorset. He lived at that time, as, indeed, he does still, in the small smuggling village of East Chaldon which lies hidden some three miles inland from the wild stretch of coast between Lulworth and Weymouth.

I remained well through that autumn. I continued to take

enormous walks in all weathers, scrambling about the high chalk cliffs with the sea-blown rain lashing against my face. I came to know every rock, every high guillemot ledge, every projecting promontory. Sometimes on clear nights my brother and I would walk together to an old stone circle situated on the shoulder of the downs above the village called Poxwell, or Puck's Well, as it should more properly be written. And standing there in the centre of that grey Druidic ring we would listen to the surge of the distant sea, peering up, meanwhile, at the great Square of Pegasus, like two conjured spirits with red beards wagging.

As I still coughed it was now suggested that in order "to finish my cure" I had better pay one more visit to Switzerland. This time I selected to go to the small winter resort of Arosa. On my arrival I found that I had a slight temperature and in consequence lay still for a few days. However, I soon grew impatient, and, excusing the fever on account of the rarefied air, once more took to walking. With the help of a pair of Canadian snowshoes I was able to leave the paths and climb along the higher mountain slopes.

Now, it happened one day, as I was carelessly looking at a map of Switzerland hung up in the hotel vestibule, that I was astounded to observe the word Davos-Platz almost touching that of Arosa and, on examining the map more closely, found out that, although by train the two places were separated by a twenty-four-hour journey, as the crow flies only some fifteen miles of mountain lay between them. Indeed, I realised that I had actually been looking at the other side of "Queen Victoria 'curing'" each afternoon as I sat taking tea on the hotel balcony. The discovery affected me like one of those dreams when familiar places, far distant from each other, suddenly merge; when the hard walls of a gravel school-yard, let us say, open unaccountably into the paddock of one's home. The mountain opposite now began to obsess my imagination. I found myself continually stopping in front of the map to study the minute topographical markings near the words Furka Pass. It was fascinating to me to know that I was looking at the other side of that range, every contour of which had been indelibly printed on my memory. I kept imagining myself coming down off the very slopes whose beauty, as seen from my bed, had so often beguiled the end of a long afternoon. I made up my mind to cross the mountain range.

The day I selected for the adventure was cloudless. I confided my purpose to no one. I took some sandwiches with me, and walking slowly and steadily soon found myself above the timber-line and confronted by smooth sheets of sparkling virginal snow. The crows in the dark trees below croaked a warning, but I gave no heed to them. The actual Furka Pass, as I remember, was about fifty feet wide, a steep slope of snow that went down into I knew not what abyss. However, by stamping I could break through the frozen crust and in this way secure a firm footing. Once across I found myself on a mountain plateau surrounded by rocky peaks. All was glinting white, all was silent. No track of animal traversed that high expanse, no flight of bird was seen to pass across the blue ether. I did meet with one live thing—a tortoiseshell butterfly! It came fluttering over those eternal snows with the light carelessness characteristic of this particular species, and which may perhaps account for the fact that one so often sees them, with wings frayed, tragically imprisoned against the dusty coloured-glass of church windows. I kept looking up at the sky. I very well recognised the danger of being caught in a snow-storm. On I went over that high mountain level, leaving behind me a strange webbed track, as though some fabulous grebe had waddled across the white plateau. I was very excited. Would I ever reach the other side? I felt my pulse. It was racing. And as each hour passed I became more and more conscious of the hot flush of my sickness tingling under my skin. Had I undertaken too much? And then suddenly I was rewarded! I had come to the top of the last ridge and there, far down below, across the valley, stood Clavadel Sanatorium, fretted with balconies, and looking like a doll's house against that stupendous landscape. I was exultant. I walked along in an ecstasy. Well I knew that I was passing over those cusped slopes which a year ago had seemed to me as remote as the furthest rose-tinted cloud. I found my way down to the timber and before long came upon a chalet where mountain hay had been stored. A woodcutter's path led from this remote barn so that in half an hour I was in the Frauenkirk village.

I hired a room in the little inn and made my way slowly up to the Sanatorium. The dinner-gong had sounded and the patients had already collected in the spacious dining-room, each corner of which had been made so neatly concave. My appearance seemed miraculous, my story unbelievable. With my face burned to an unhealthy blazing red I walked from one familiar group to another; the young German doctor, in his white coat, following me about and asking me to explain to him by what new method I had cured myself. And all the time while I received their congratulations I could feel my heart knocking against the walls of my ribs. Before long I left the noisy hall and stepped out into the cold moonlight which, with so curious an effect, was illumined by those sad flaunting windows.

Once back in the little inn I went to bed. I flooded the room with frosty air and lay down to sleep. I could not sleep. Nervous thoughts kept scurrying through my skull like mice in a pantry. Hour after hour went by, and then what I had been unconsciously anticipating actually happened. With a wretched sinking at the pit of my stomach I suddenly recognised the intolerable *bubbling sensation* in my chest indicative of a hæmorrhage. I turned on the light, hoping against hope. I coughed, I looked, and once more I saw blood. Slowly the dawn came. News of my relapse was sent to Clavadel and a black sleigh arrived to carry me back to the Sanatorium, the greatest fool in all that dolorous citadel.

Over a month elapsed before I was strong enough to travel back to England. For a year after this I remained at home following out a rigid routine of life and in this way managing to hold my sickness in check. The summer of 1912, however, again found me on the Continent. This time I visited Italy with my brother John. We stayed in Venice. During those strangely exciting weeks I never for a moment was unaware of the presence of my dread complaint. When before breakfast I strolled out into the garden for the pleasure of watching the lizards chase each other behind the rose bushes trained to grow against the hot white wall of the hotel I knew of it. And again I knew of it when during languid summer nights we drifted along the canals with dark water, so startlingly evocative of the smells of an obscure antiquity, lapping against the bottom of our gondola and against the green-stained masonry of walls and stairways, the support-ing piles of which had been laid in place on the muddy rush-grown bottom of an open lagoon, so many years ago. On one occasion I saw a young Venetian girl, her head covered with a black lace shawl, eating a bunch of red currants on the steps of a marble palace, and even then I did not forget; no, nor when, from the merciless meshes of a fisherman's net, I disentangled the hard crinkled body of a sea-horse, so exquisitely manufactured, and now left to perish on hot Adriatic sands.

Very well I remember, also at this time, sitting on a seat with Louis Wilkinson, listening to his wise saws about death coming to all of us and it being absurd to worry whether it came late or soon.

From Venice we went to Milan and put up at the Hôtel Roma. Tired after the journey I took a hot bath, always an unwise thing for a consumptive to do. In a quarter of an hour I was once more coughing up blood. For weeks I lay on my back unable to move. To add to my misery I underwent a severe attack of kidney stone. This was the first time I had been a sufferer from this disorder and I was amazed at the pain I had to endure. It was like having a rat gnawing at your entrails. Fortunately a most civilised Italian doctor was quite prepared to inject me with as much morphia as I wanted. He was the first doctor to say that I might live for years if, as he added, I gave up "climbing mountains." He confided to me that his own age was sixty-five. "Sixty-five!" he said, "that is not very nice for me," and he gave me the dry look of a philosopher.

Apparently the houses across the street from my hotel were occupied by light women of the town. I used to watch them tiring themselves at their mirrors all through the hot summer afternoons. It was depressing to contemplate the shallow monotony of their existence. Sometimes one or other of them would come to the window and look out in the direction of the Cathedral, and I used to wonder in what manner they regarded that ornamental monument which had known so many of their kind pace backwards and forwards over the echoing paving-stones so far below its spiral pinnacles. I had no idea that the girls had marked my presence or troubled their dilatory heads about me one way or the other. However, when the doctor at length allowed me to get up they crowded to their windowsills like so many coloured birds in an aviary and began clapping their hands, overjoyed at my recovery. I waved and threw kisses at each one of them in turn. I don't believe I have ever received a demonstration of affection that has touched me more to the heart than this display from these daughters-of-joy, the tedium and frivolity of whose existence I had been witnessing for so many weeks.

We sailed from Genoa, calling at Lisbon. I wanted to visit the grave of Henry Fielding, but did not dare to go on shore, having caught a dysentery at Tangiers. I did not leave England again till 1914. Once more I concentrated my whole attention upon fighting my sickness, resting and regulating my walks and being nourished with bowls of fresh creamy milk, the rich produce of the half-dozen cows I used to watch each summer moving placidly about through buttercups and shadowed grass, as I lay on my boy-scout bed at the top of the terrace walk not far from the phloxes, the fragrance of which on sultry August afternoons, always seems to suggest, in its delicate luxuriance, the sun-warmed velvet-soft abdomens of peacock butterflies. The farmer's wife across the lane used to give me every few days a basket of fresh turkeys' eggs. I must have consumed a countless number of these eggs. I would make a tiny hole at one end of their mottled shells and suck them with all the care and dainty precision of a punctilious weasel. In spite of my pains, however, my complaint seemed to gain ground. An old man in the village who had at one time been our coachman advised me to rub my chest with goose grease. I procured a pot of this precious ointment and my sister Gertrude every night would dress me with it as I lay in my bed under the stars. Often on these occasions we would remain quite still listening, listening to the distant barking of some dog who had heard the muffled footsteps of a traveller on the turnpike road, listening to the calling of a corncrake in the neighbouring field "put up for hay," listening to the singular sound made by a hedgehog in its prickly advance from one flower-bed to another.

Alas! Goose grease and turkey eggs proved of small avail. I grew worse. My brother Willie now wrote from Africa begging me to come out to him. It seemed risky, but not more risky than staying where I was. I left the port of London in September 1914, having spent my last week in bed with blood-spitting, a condition which at that time seemed to have become almost chronic with me.

I sailed round Africa by the Cape of Good Hope, my zest for life seeming to be keener than ever as I handled the flying fish which in the early morning would sometimes get stranded on the deck near where I lay. I used to stand at the end of the vessel and watch an albatross which followed our course, sweeping backwards and forwards with tireless white wings outspread. and then I would cough, and as the morsel of coloured spittle was caught in the dark rollers of that vast ocean over which the bird was flying, I would marvel at the tenacity of this sickness which it was my destiny to carry about with me to the ends of the world.

The altitude of the highlands of Kenya where my brother lived was 7,000 feet above sea level and the air in consequence, baked by the tropical sun, was very dry. My condition responded immediately to the change of climate. I was in Africa for five years and during all that time I never spent a day in bed. I still coughed, still expectorated, but in spite of all the hardships incident to a pioneer's life I continued, out of all reason, to remain well.

Once back in England I bought a revolving shelter. I had it

hauled by a farm wagon up to the deserted overgrown garden of a ruined cottage situated on the crest of the hill called Jordan which lies to the east of Weymouth. Like a hermit I lived in this shelter for a year, walking down to the town each night for my dinner, but returning to my lonely habitation before midnight. In the early mornings I would wake to look upon a small still bay with rocks and rippling pools. Little hedge birds would begin to twitter on the grey stone wall near the empty nettle-filled well, while over a restless sea, behind the outline of a corn-field, black hungry cormorants would follow each other on their way to their distant feeding-places. I was in England for a year.

On the 13th of August, the thirty-sixth anniversary of my birthday, I sailed with my brother to America. The first winter spent by me in New York was encouraging. We lived at that time on Twenty-first Street opposite the Anglican Seminary in old Chelsea. Each night I would carry my mattress on to the roof. From first to last I have derived extraordinary satisfaction and consolation from sleeping on the roofs of New York houses. What a sweet restorative influence resides in those dim aerial spaces above the great city! How unspeakably refreshing after the racket of the streets, or after contact with shallow society people, to emerge through a trap-door into a dark inaccessible region under the stars! One comes to know the chimneys as if they were trees, sheltering now behind this one, now behind that, according to the quarter from which the wind is blowing. Rain would always wake me; but I found I often continued to sleep after it had begun to snow, opening my eyes to discover the roof and my own blankets hidden under a cold fleecy coverlet. Sometimes very early, in a faint grey light, sea-gulls would pass rapidly overhead. Indeed, I know of few things that I have found more liberating to my imagination than the sight of a common gull crossing the sky above a great city at the hour before dawn.

The following summer I spent with my brother in California. We stayed at Sausalito. A week after our arrival we walked over the downs to the Pacific Ocean. I was full of eagerness to dip my hands into its waters. It was a hot day, and although our walk was a happy one, with spring flowers thick upon the sloping hills, it proved too much for me. I began once more to spit blood. George Stirling persuaded me to take electrical treatments from Dr. Abrams. I was conducted to this modern Faustus by the poet himself. The "doctor" impressed me. I judged him to be half a charlatan and half a genius. I received ten treatments and was dismissed as cured. I suspected his verdict—you cannot catch old birds with chaff! But apparently the treatments did do me good. However, by the beginning of 1924 I was once more suffering from a slight evening fever. In the month of May I accepted an invitation to go hunting grizzly bears in the Rocky Mountains. I saw much that interested me. I saw a porcupine nibbling at the broad horn that a moose had shed and which was lying on the sun-warmed pine needles. I saw a bitch badger bringing her young down to drink in a mountain stream. I saw bears; I saw elk and moose and, indeed, received a hundred intimate glimpses of nature so refreshing to a countryman who for long months has been in a city.

I got back safely to New York, but as the days passed it became more and more evident that the camp food, the hard riding, and perhaps still more my immoderate love of walking, had done damage that it would take months to repair. I left for the country. Before I had reached my destination, however, I had a hæmorrhage. Being unwilling to attract the attention of my fellow-passengers I kept as still and silent as I could. My eyes would look out at rock-strewn Connecticut meadows drowsy in the summer sunshine. On my birthday I sent a cable to my brother in England to show him that I had at any rate reached forty years. And I must confess as I lay in bed looking over the Norwalk garden trees, to where the masts of a schooner so unexpectedly appeared through green foliage, I found that my distaste for dying was as strong in middle life as ever it was in my youth. I want to live to a great old age like my father and grandfather and my great-grandfather before me. I want to live till "the grasshopper has become a burden." Indeed, if I could have my way, I would still be about on the 13th of August 1984, still able to look up at the great Square of Pegasus with all the unregenerate egoism of one who from childhood recognised that however prolonged his life might be, it would pass as swiftly as the flight of a gull crossing from horizon to horizon of a marine city in the hour before dawn.

THE PARTRIDGE

IN one of his short essays, William Barnes, the Dorset poet, makes reference to the sensation of pure happiness that will be sometimes present with a man who is working in a garden. A fortnight ago I experienced this sensation. It was during one of those protracted white twilights that follow the longest day, and a stillness lay upon the green valleys, delicate and profound. I was occupied in planting out seedling lettuces, but because of the beauty of the evening I found myself constantly compelled to pause and contemplate the large peace of the downs as the summer night gathered over them. The smell of dew was in the air, the smell of that wild water that God distils for the refreshment of His common weeds. A few stars were already visible in the vast concave of the darkening sky. No human being could possibly have been indifferent to these momentary periods of eternity. The living grass, the breathing cattle, the religious piece-work labourers, seemed to have been rescued, to have been saved, by some immortal exemption, by some God-like benediction.

All at once near to me I heard the cry of a partridge. Its cry was insistent, and suggested an utter mastery of those secret laws by which these birds have preserved their species down the centuries. Through the cool air it came, again and again, that reiterated call—Perdix! Perdix! Perdix!

The cry suggested an awareness of the hour, of this hour of mystical grace. I could not doubt that the bird, with its sharp vision, was cognisant of the fairy dusk, as it kept summoning its companion to her sleep in a tone of anxious reassurance, in a tone such as might have been used by the sire of corn elves, calling together an errant brood astray in bindweed jungles.

To be alive, only to be alive! Here is the praise, the wonder, and the glory! Far off over the hills a dog was barking. Above my head a bat flickered; while against the dim clouds, uttering its dolorous deep-sea cry, a herring gull was flying with concentrated purpose towards the chalk cliffs. Could anything be more mysterious, more miraculous than life?—this dog domesticated out of all recognition of its primitive estate; this shrill mouse fitted so neatly with precise diminutive wings, hooked and outstretched like those of a pigmy devil; and this proud bird, a lonely wayfarer above the square inland meadows. Surely the worship of the hour carried a sublime assurance that all was well, that good hope lay at the bottom.

So sustained was the tranquillity of the evening that one might fancy it an interval set apart by God for His own praying time, and that one might accidentally surprise Him "in his piety" in any of the valleys, His mighty spirit disordered by misgivings, by compassion! Moment by moment, moment by moment, night was falling. Surely, surely it engulfed an earth innocent of guile, an earth where the lamb could lie down with the lion, and the sucking child be at ease with the cockatrice. Always the partridge kept calling—Perdix! Perdix! Perdix! There was anxiety at the back of the call, but it was the anxiety of the felicity of absolute love. Wishing to see where the bird was, I climbed over the fence. Suddenly, from under my very feet, the hen got up. I had almost trodden on her nest. So this was the explanation of the male bird's clamour. I could just make out the eggs upon which she had been sitting. She could hardly have selected a more precarious position for her nest. It was on the side of a ditch along which the pony in the home plot was always grazing, and where the cats were fond of hunting. I got back into the garden, hoping that somehow or another she would manage to prove that the selection of such a site was not ill-considered.

Ten days went by and each day I watched her. She did not fly up if I kept some five yards away, and from this distance I could, through the tall cocksfoot grasses, easily detect her form, a prone body, soft and brown. I was utterly amazed by her constancy, by the silent determined devotion of this game bird who carried on her breast the lucky gipsy design of a chestnut-coloured horseshoe! What could possess her to remain motionless on these few inches of prison ground? Why did she not, with self-interested abandon, run free over the fields, peering beneath shadowed leaves for the victuals of her choice, picking up ants' eggs, morsels of grain, eager and blithe.

To see her day after day so obedient gave the impression of an utter goodness, an entire spiritual subjection to a purpose irrelevant to her own personal life, a subjection purged of self-advantage. Each night, punctual as the evening star, I would hear the male bird begin his confederate chatter—Perdix! Perdix! Perdix! It was odd to think of this intimate association between two living creatures, so close to us, so far from us, of two living creatures with beating hearts, hearing ears, seeing eyes—creatures capable of narrowly watching the deliberate displacement of a horse's hoof from a tussock of grass.

Every day I expected her young to be hatched. I knew that as soon as the shells crack fledgeling partridges are able to stand up, to walk, to run. I have seen them in full flight down a cart rut, eggshell fragments still adhering to their quick chicken bodies.

Then there came a night of darkness when the moon was not due to rise till the small hours of the morning. It began to rain, and I was reminded of those sinister nights in Africa when lions boldly raid cattle camps. The currant bushes, so harmless in the day-time, took to themselves now a darkly massed, dangerous look. It was a night when evil might well triumph without miscarriage. And in the ditch near the lettuce bed evil did triumph. A rat, old and crafty, found the bird. By chance I heard her, the sound of her fluttering, and ran down to the place. I managed to catch the partridge up and carried her, all wet and trembling, into the kitchen. In the horrible scuffle she had lost many of her feathers, and one side of her breast had been punctured. Yet as I held her in my hand she still seemed full of life. Her eye was bright and I could feel her start and quiver. I decided to take her into the middle of the field. If I found she could neither walk nor fly, then I would kill her. In my hands under the light of a candle she no longer looked dutiful and dedicated. She appeared very young and very sensitive. She suggested a maiden whose secret life-illusion has suffered some hideous violation. When I put her down on the grass she soon disappeared, rushing off into the darkness with a frantic sidelong action in the direction of her nest.

I never saw her again. I broke one of her eggs and found the miniature bird already matted with feathers, a golden ring about its tiny grotesque nape. The struggle had rendered the hiding-place open to all eyes, utterly exposed. The nest had been razed, and like the locality of a murder, the atmosphere under the overhanging nettles seemed still to retain a fearful impression of what had occurred—the nature-entranced bird silently sitting in the rough ditch, her task nearing its completion; the soothing summer rain pattering down upon her small intelligent head as she was suddenly confronted by the hyæna physiognomy of a dunghill rat, foul, and fierce, and resolute to kill.

The eggs are now all broken, and a dock is coming up in the centre of the nest's floor. All is forgotten, all cancelled by death in the strong drift of advancing time which draws all happenings back into oblivion. And yet the incident is not utterly over, for every night at the hour of twilight, at that hour when the cattle cease from grazing, and the swallow sleeps, and the owl wakes, I hear the solicitous love-call of the cock bird as, with his triangular feet, he circuitously approaches the ill-chosen ditch.

Each night he has been there, a deluded and distracted lover giving a monotonous utterance to his one simple sentence—"Perdix! Perdix! Perdix! Perdu! Perdu! Perdu!"

ON THE OTHER SIDE OF THE
QUANTOCKS

When we were children, no holiday excursion gave us more happiness than a day spent on the Quantocks. These moorland hills, rising north-west from Taunton and stretching almost to the Bristol Channel, were very exciting to us. I suppose their attraction depended largely upon the nature of their scenery, which was utterly different from that of our home. We were used enough to South Somerset, with its clay and mud,—"bad for the rider, good for the bider,"— whereas these wild Ishmaelitic hills possessed the charm of the unfamiliar.

The other day, after an interval of a quarter of a century, I saw them again. The occasion that impelled me this time was a sad one. I went to visit the grave of a girl who, during the cold weeks of last January, had died at the old fishing village of Watchet and had been buried there. A particular poignancy attended this death. She had left us at the New Year to look for a house in the West Country. She and her husband had found a place that suited them exactly, and were about to return to London to make the final arrangements incident to their new life, when, after an illness of only two days, she was dead.

I have been told that the Chinese emphasise a difference between ordinary partings and these other particular partings when, in our ignorance of the crooked ways of fate, we separate from those we love for ever. It is their rumour also that an approaching death will cast a forward shadow.

It certainly seems to me in retrospect that when I last saw her I had had an obscure premonition of what was to happen. She was suffering from a cold, and, lying in the corner of a wide cottage bed, she looked alarmingly fragile. I remember also that there came to me, as I walked back over the downs, certain chance glimpses of her in the past, glimpses that presented themselves as distinctly as pictures. I saw her waiting beside the standing August corn, her hand shading her eyes. I saw her in the seaweed pool at the bottom of the White Nose; and again I saw her by the fireside gravely quoting to me this lilt she had learned from her mother:—

> "The best bed's a feather bed,
> The best bed of all.
> The next bed is a bed
> Made of pea straw.
> The pea straw is dirty,
> It will dirty all your gown;
> But never mind the feather bed,
> Lay yourself down."

Her life had not been a completely happy one. The same intensity that gave so high a quality to her writing made it hard for her to fortify herself against the thwartings and disappointments of the years. Her spirit was as vulnerable as her body, with its bones light as the bones of a bird. She always remained a child, and if she stood on highest tiptoe could never measure more than a hogweed in a hedge.

As is so often the case with the very young, the agitations of her soul would communicate themselves directly to her body, so that if you were holding her hand when she was troubled, you would feel it vibrant and trembling like a minnow freshly taken from the net.

I set out on my expedition proposing to spend my first night at Crowcombe, a small village which lies at the foot of the Quantocks, and from there, the next day, to walk over the moors to Watchet. I found the village unchanged; the old red-brick Court House of the Carew family standing just as I remembered it, and to the right of the church the same steep lane leading on to the hills.

I took a room at the Carew Arms and had tea before a wide old-fashioned fireplace. As I ate my meal of whortle-berry jam and Devonshire cream I seemed for the first time fully to appreciate the satisfaction that Hazlitt felt on those rare occasions when he was known to the world by no nearer definition than "the gentleman in the parlour." After I had finished I made up my mind to climb the Quantocks that very evening in order to discover the best route for my walk the following day.

Of all the lanes in the world this Crowcombe lane charms me most. I had never gone up it before in the spring-time, and in this opening period of the year the mossy track seemed more beautiful even than I had remembered. There were periwinkles out on the crumbling walls and everywhere primroses. The lane wound upward and upward under the most splendid beech trees. The enormous trunks of these trees, rising with silent might out of the bare ground, their horizontally interlacing branches lifted higher and ever higher, awoke the spirit to the worship of Nature's strength, to the worship of her patient piety. The mute boughs, still winter-bare and yet united into one harmony, were to the eye as organ music to the ear. It seemed that not one grey-white outspreading branch had changed its form since the days of my childhood, since that dog-day morning when, as a small boy, I had followed my Aunt Dora up the steep path, trying my best with a frond of bracken to beat away the stinging flies that troubled her. I had been impatient then to reach the top of the lane, and on this spring night the same urge was upon me. Not Table Mountain, not Mount Tamalpais, not Kenya, not Mount Carmel, not Vesuvius, not one of them all had stolen the old appeal of the West Country hill.

At last I was on the summit and looking with corporeal eye at this prospect, which on so many different occasions, in places so far from Crowcombe, had been present to the inward vision of my mind. Under the bright cold sky of that April evening I could see the hills in all their glory, fold beyond fold, combe below combe, falling away to the western ocean. On the farthest horizon it was possible to make out the mountains of Wales, while in the mid-distance, set in the silver sea of the Bristol Channel, was the island of Steep Holmes standing black against the water, black against the parrot-green nursery meadows that slope down to the very shore.

Always as children we had longed to see a red deer. In vain we had searched for one, diligently exploring each grove of stunted oak trees, pushing our way through every patch of bracken that seemed dense or secluded. We had followed the mountain streams from one rocky basin to another, but on no single occasion had we disturbed hind or stag. Now after all these years my luck had changed, for as I walked through the heather stalks blackened with fire I suddenly became aware that two of these animals had risen not fifty yards away. They were so large that almost I could imagine myself back in the highlands of Africa looking at water-buck. For a moment they remained motionless, gazing at me with the concentrated attention characteristic of wild life suddenly disturbed by man, as though even in these latter days the appearance of our kind, erect and biped, still had something startling about it, something that demanded a more exact ocular investigation than an ordinary object in nature. Then in an instant they were away over the next ridge, their antlers clear-cut against the sky, moving with a succession of absolutely silent leaps, as animals in a dream, as beasts on a tapestry come miraculously to life.

I have often noticed that any particularly favoured sight of Nature's more perfect disciplines is apt to remove for a certain time those limitations of perception that use and wont so quickly impose upon us. Without warning, without reason, we find ourselves suddenly able to experience emotions roaming and marginal, to see life with the eye of Merlin. This happened to me now as I rested on a heap of dry heather half-way down the lane, at the very spot where as a boy I had lost my silver birthday watch among the whortleberries.

Night was already falling. Never had I seen the planet Venus more beautiful, never had I seen her shine with a light more firm. As I looked at her in her isolated loveliness, the heels of my boots pressing into the soft mould of the familiar earth, and with my senses enmeshed in mystery, suddenly there was the sound of church bells upon the twilight air. It was at that moment as if this Christian sound coming up from the village below belonged really and truly to another world, a world without sorrow or death, a world no longer rude, a world where love was as gentle as mill-stream flowers and as eternal as light. Up through the naked beech tree branches came the sound as from a great distance, the fitful cadence of its tintinnabulation borne, now soft, now loud, upon the restless winds of the wood.

All Christmas nights were in the sound and all New Year Eves. It tolled for the passing of the souls of all men, of all women; it chimed for the wedding processions of true lovers

32

who for centuries have slept dreamless far under the roots of red-berried yew trees. Now it sounded dolorous as the stroke of a harbour bell giving warning of danger in the dusk of an autumn evening; now happy as a chime from the turret of a chapel, when cuckoo-flowers and kingcups are out in the water meadows, and the prince and princess at play in their garden bower.

It was as though these bell clappers were truly ancient mediæval tongues telling of days out of the past; telling of antique cradles, of the enchanted web of flaxen sheets grey with age; telling of churchyards still prosperous and emerald bright, but where the strife of this naughty world has been for ever cancelled, and where the knight and his lady have been lying without lust for a period without computation, and where the rook boy elbows the goose girl and the hen wife the swineherd with ugly brown teeth. It was a music out of the past. It told of what might have been and never has been; a music of the very borderland of the wilful senses; a music of a paradise serene and glad, where impassioned phantoms wander free, their minds, their bodies, at peace at last.

When I waked the next morning it was raining. "You are never going on to the hills today," remarked my hostess as she brought in my breakfast. However, by the time I had reached the top of the lane the day had begun to improve.

Hidden among some trees I came upon a small hut. I knocked on its door. A rough man appeared, and I asked him which of the tracks would bring me to Watchet. He rubbed his sandy grey hair and looked suspiciously at me. He was large-boned and unkempt, and his boots were unlaced. Eventually he gave me the directions I wanted. I stood talking to him. He had lived in his small house all his life. He made a livelihood by fetching away the carcasses of the deer killed by the hounds, and distributing the venison among the farmers and village people. For the performance of this task he had a cart and a small tough pony; and he assured me that, knowing the moors as he did, and the habits of the red deer, he scarcely ever failed to be in at the death. He told me that his name was Truggins. What the correct word in the lore of venery would be to describe a man with his duties I do not know.

I now made my way along the high ridge that lies to the west of the hills, and a proud walk it is over this shoulder of the Quantocks. To the left the traveller looks down upon the lowlands that separate them from Dunkery Beacon. The ploughed fields showed the red tilth characteristic of Devonshire, and the meadows were small and regular as chess-board squares. I came upon a weather-beaten, weather-bitten thorn tree standing by itself in a place where five grassy tracks met. Judging from the size of its trunk, it must have been of a great age. It was hoar with crisp crinkled lichen, but I noticed that every twig was decorated with living buds. It was difficult to imagine this ancient hawthorn in flower, its twisted besom branches soft with the opulent sweetness of May.

What a trysting-place this tree would make! Almost certainly it had before now been used for this recurring human need, perhaps by Ruth herself before ever she had come to wander mad and was observed by William Wordsworth trifling with her toys in the brown trout streams.

> "That oaten pipe of hers is mute,
> Or thrown away; but with a flute
> Her loneliness she cheers:

This flute, made of a hemlock stalk,
At evening in his homeward walk
  The Quantock woodman hears.

I, too, have passed her on the hills
Setting her little water-mills
  By spouts and fountains wild—
Such small machinery as she turned
Ere she had wept, ere she had mourned,
  A young and happy Child!"

I came down from the Quantocks at their north-western extremity to discover that I still had several miles to walk before reaching Watchet. The hotel where Ann Reid had died was an old and attractive building. The proprietor and his wife had done all within their power to help her. I looked at these good people with gratitude, selected as they had been out of all the population of England to cherish the last hours of this girl's life. They showed me her room. It was an ordinary hotel bedroom, but I noticed that between the roofs of the houses across the street a wide space of open sky must have been visible from her pillow. It has always seemed to me no inconsequent matter what our eyes look upon in the hour of death. It was garden birds twittering in the clematis outside her window that made up my mother's last impression of earth life.

I walked to the churchyard on the hill. There was the grave under the farther wall, with the mould still showing raw and with strips of green turf laid unevenly on the mound.

The church of Watchet is dedicated to St. Decuman. It stands on the summit of a hill midway between Exmoor and the Quantocks. The body of the church is hidden by trees, but its tower is visible from a great distance like a kind of

Glastonbury Tor rising by itself. I was happy to know that she who had always been so steadfast a champion of the spiritually oppressed should have her burial plot marked by so brave a sign.

When all has been said, how abject a grave can look! "We are the dead"—"We are the dead"—"We are the dead!" Yet out of the dumb ground there rose no word of reproach. "Every day, every hour that you breathe you experience a miracle. You are still free and alive. Brief as a rainbow your dream also will be. There is no clemency, no reprieve, no escape; no, not for the strongest heart deep mortised in life. 'A straw, a hair hath done it.'"

A POND

A MILE from my cottage there is a small pond. It lies in the centre of a triangular lawn where two valleys meet. Except for the old shepherd, nobody knows of it. Though it has the beautiful shape of a dew pond, it is not one. It is only a common pond supplied by the surface water of the wide downland gorges, and yet it has always seemed to me to be enchanted. I have often thought, as I have passed by it, that one day, under a special dispensation, I should receive from this little pool of water, from this small, green stoup of lustral water, a whisper as to the secret of life. It will be revealed to me, I have thought, as surely and as naturally as the presence of dew makes itself felt on folded twilight flowers found suddenly damp to the touch after the dry butterfly periods of a summer's day.

Always hoping for this hour of grace, I have loitered by the pond's edge at every season. I have observed with accuracy the changes that come over its surface. All through the winter months its waters are clear, but in the spring-time the pond-buttercups grow up and afford a vegetable screen for the dabbling unrest of the newts, those little ancestors with orange bellies and gilded eyes who are privileged to experience the forgotten rhythm of saurian life. In summer the pond becomes green-mantled, the ranunculus disappears, and its place is taken by duckweed, with tiny, floating, sequin-round leaves. It is then that the tadpoles turn into frogs, and it is possible to catch one of these diminutive, yellow-green basilisks and set it upon the back of one's hand to watch its globular throat blow in and out, until with a headlong leap it has escaped into the long grass.

A few seconds' scrutiny of a frog, in all its perfection, corrects us of that gross apathy with which we too often approach the miracle of our fugitive existence. Use and wont make all life a commonplace thing. Our ordinary minds demand an ordinary world and feel at ease only when they have explained and taken for granted the mysteries among which we have been given so short a licence to breathe. Imagine the state of wonder that would possess our spirits had we been suddenly transported to the earth from some planet undisturbed by the urge of life. We should exclaim as much over a little hip-frog as over a thumb-high whelp of a hippogriff surprised under a dock leaf. We should then no longer be blind to the planet's mystery latent in wood and stone. A sea-gull's feather picked up would shock us into the excitement we now should feel at finding the pinion of an errant cherubim. We should stand still as a stock to contemplate so slender a quill of air-filled horn which, with its filaments of adhering thistledown, can fan the heavy bodies of animals buoyant through the air. At every step we took we should be startled afresh.

We should sit at the sea's margin only to learn that the summer waves, dancing like lambs against the congregated beaches, were peopled with legless animals silver-plated, and with the gift of flashing motion. The astonishment we should feel at seeing a cheap ant would keep us on our knees before the galleried citadels of the pismires till nightfall. Can it be possible that insects, scarcely as large as grass seeds, are diligently obedient to laws of a civil polity? And a butterfly seen for the first time—what spectacle so delicate? A painted-lady on a scabious, under the bewitchment of a love more dainty-sweet than the concupiscence of toadstool fairies!

The West Chaldon shepherd told me once that he had seen the ghost of a cow walk into the pond and vanish. "There were no stock on down at the time, and a' vanished from my eyes as quick as fox in fern." I was not surprised by this rumour. The pond was a charmed pond. I had always known it. It is a mirror that reflects God's moving shadow.

It was on a soft evening of this last September that there came to me the breath of the knowledge I sought. Beneath the sky the downs raised their patient shoulders with noble simplicity. Recumbent cattle could not have imparted to the mood of that hour a deeper peace. The last rays of the sun touched to brightest silver the fluff of the thistles withered and brown. All was silent, all was expectant. The messenger for whom I had waited was at last revealed.

It was a hare. I saw her from far away and did not so much as venture to move a finger. She approached with uncertain steps—now advancing, now retreating, now frolicsome, now grave. The secret nature of the hills seemed during those suspended moments to be open to her sensitive spirit. A tender light was on the swaying grass ends through which the russet creature, with elf-high ears, gambolled. Nearer and nearer she came. Was she actually intending to drink? Was it possible that I should see her lower her soft brown chin to the water within ten yards of me? Surely if I were permitted to witness so delicate an operation, then at last I should receive the revelation I sought. The stillness of the evening was so profound that the fur of a field mouse's jacket brushing against the stems of its grassy jungle would have been audible, while against the sky, infinitely remote, the moon hung in an utter calm.

This hour in the downland valley was, I knew well, but of

an inconsequent second's duration in the moon's age-long espionage of the earth's physical being. She had seen the magical and molten ash of the earth's orb stirred with the trouble of life. She had seen passionate men, resolute and adroit, raise themselves out of the dust. She had heard them cry out to the gods whose thoroughfares are uncatalogued star spaces. She had seen them go stumbling through lucky grass, their hearts distraught with love. She herself was part of the profound mystery of the humming firmament, the outer rim of which, for a few scattered moments, has been envisaged by the dreaming minds of men. The truth resides in matter's proud processions as they are revealed to our uncertain senses. In what can be seen, in what can be heard, in what can be touched, tasted, and felt, there is no treason. Only these messengers can be trusted. Here are the golden threads which alone can lead us without betrayal to those true states of beatific vision, ephemeral and sublime, wherein through the medium of our vulgar faculties we may see immortal movement, bright and clear, upon our planet.

I was suddenly awakened from my rapture. I had heard a sound, a sound sensitive and fresh as soft rain upon a leaf. It was the hare drinking.

THE SHAMBLES FOG-HORN

WHEREVER you live there is always some predominating sound that seems to give expression to the mood of the particular district. In the springtime in country places it is perhaps the song of the lark which, in the early hours of the dawn, charms us back to consciousness during those suspended moments when we are half awake and half asleep.

Shakespeare was indulging in no poetic fancy when he described these birds as "ploughman's clocks," for it is their trilling incantations that first break the religious stillness of the night when darkness still lies over the streets and fields and the light is not yet. The first sound of animate life invariably is from this bird. I hear it before the gulls rise from their roosting ledges, before the cuckoo asserts his irresponsible affirmation.

In cities now-a-days it is too often the hooting of a factory that sends its harsh reverberation far up to where clouds drift free over our house-tops. Sometimes, however, in favoured towns like Sherborne, it is the sound of church bells that welcomes in the day, reminding us with their strange and beautiful music of the flowing away of our priceless hours. Heard from a distance, when safe from the sense of depression that falls upon some of us with the thought of conventional church-going, this music is of all music perhaps the most moving, with its mediæval appeal and its suggestion of the pathos of the human heart. Charles

Lamb used to consider that the sound of church bells was nearest that marginal other world for which in times of distress and bereavement we so desperately long.

What a lovely object a bell is, with the simplicity of its shell-like curves and its suspended wagging tongue! A spiritual power has been attributed to this human invention from time out of mind. The original idea of tolling a bell in the hour of death was to frighten away the malevolent bat-like devils reputed to be invisibly present over every town and village. The passing knell would begin and immediately these wicked flocks would scatter, and for a short period a passage would be clear for the ghost, released from its prison of flesh.

It is not, however, the lark, or a factory hooter, or abbey bells that give an especial sound-character to the district that lies inland from that noble line of cliffs to the east of Weymouth. From Redcliff Bay, from the Black Nore, from Ringstead, from the White Nose, from Bats Head, from Swyre Head, and even from as far as Rings Hill, the sound that dominates our senses comes from the sea. It is intermittent; for weeks together we may not hear it, but so deep an impression has it made upon our senses that it is always in our minds, has become, as it were, an experience permanently anticipated. It is a sound of warning. It possesses a dread power. It is the articulation of enduring far-sighted man confronting the turbulence of ruthless Nature. I am referring to the moaning of the Shambles lightship fog-horn. Whenever the sea-frit gathers about the cliffs obliterating them from sight, one after the other, as it drifts over the sloping "bottoms," then we begin unconsciously to mark our moments by this rhythmic booming coming in from the Channel.

It is exciting to think of this stoutly built, tub-like craft moored fast to those sinister submarine rocks, month after month, year after year. We feel this interest even in fair weather when the ship appears as but a speck upon the halcyon blue Channel. But in wild November storms when in the White Nose coastguard cottages it is hardly possible to hear oneself speak, when fragments of sea-weed are carried on to the cliffs several hundred feet above the raging shore, when windows are blown in and slates are sent flying from the roof like autumn leaves, what a feeling of romance comes with the sound, comes with glimpses of the ship's revolving light, a light which, because it is drawn from oil, is so much warmer than that which shows from Portland breakwater or from the end of the Bill. When for an interval the rain ceases to lash at the window-panes and for a brief moment there is a break between the ragged clouds, there the light is to be seen bravely shining; a beacon of steadfast reason and sanity amid the passion of violent nature.

Some years ago at Christmas time the weather was so bad that for weeks on end no boat could approach the gallant little ship. The marooned men wrote their Christmas letters, and putting them into a tightly sealed box, committed them to the care of the waves that went thundering past their tossing vessel. The box was picked up the next morning on the beach under Bats Head by Mr. Newberry, the wisest of all beach-combers, and the letters were transferred without delay from the care of God to the care of the Royal Mail.

When the fog-horn of the Shambles sounds it is as though some huge antediluvian monster were out searching for its lost mate through the troughs and bulging backs of the waves. On any foggy night the citizens of Weymouth who lie awake in their houses may listen to the reiterated clamour of this great beast, as it presses its slippery flat nostrils against the oolite escarpments of Portland, or lashes its way back into the Race again as if in a forlorn and lonely quest for its lost love.

THE YELLOW IRIS

In the last analysis religion can be defined as a heightened awareness of the poetry of existence. However materialistic our views become, it is consoling to know that we can never be deprived of the charmed prerogative of this devotion. The rewards of a sensitive consciousness are sufficient for the health of our spirits. If through the channels of our homely senses we learn to envisage with imagination the movement and murmur of life in our moment of time, we become confederate with eternity. With so proud a purpose before us all extravagant anthropocentric hopes appear irrelevant, and we grow content to contemplate with philosophic detachment the flux of creation as it is presented to our eyes, noses, ears, mouths, skins. All the greatest poetry from Homer to Shakespeare, from Shakespeare to John Keats, is founded upon such elementary apprehensions—apprehensions which are beyond good and evil, and which make no demand outside the curved horizons of the planet.

This morning I was awake before the sun rose. At such an hour it is easy to observe the stir of earth-life with fresh eyes. The long hours of the mysterious night, when men lie "with their heads covered," had given place to the palpable reality of another day. On all sides were revealed the phantom progressions of quick matter. Through the grey half-lit levels below the clouds herring gulls passed uttering their dolorous sea-cries. Some were breasting their way to feeding grounds far inland, others settled on an adjacent slope where, like a flock of white-breasted foreign geese, they went about carefully scanning the sod in front of their webbed feet. A chaffinch, with its air-filled bones, already responding to the approach of April, balanced its light-flitting body upon a winter cabbage intent to inspect the vegetable's broad leaves. A hare suddenly was present across the cart track, now sniffing at the ground for a trace of the passing of its blithe mate, now sitting up with long brown ears held erect. A heifer walked over the field, the forepart of her body moving with free rhythmical ease, hide and muscle and blood and bone working in perfect harmony to carry her to a near-by trough thin-slated with the transparent ice of a cold spring dawn.

Suddenly there was the sound of a human being, of a shepherd, with mouth full of oaths, come up early to the downs to drive his flock out of the acreage of roots reserved only for the night's feeding. The twilight air echoed with the barking of his dog, once again eagerly alert to his day-by-day duties after long dreaming hours alone in his dim kennel.

If we had been allowed to see the earth on the morning of its first creation we would not have been importunate to know the future, to demand that such a dispensation from non-existence should carry a promise of moral significance. "We bless thee for our creation, preservation, and all the blessings of this life" would have been our cry. Until we are satisfied with the plain miracle of life, with the plain miracle of what is, and make no further clamour, we will remain restless, froward, dissatisfied. True religion consists in a simple worship of life without stipulations. As civil spirits it is incumbent upon each one of us to resist stupidity, injustice, and cruelty; but this is no reason why we should be sentimental enough to fancy that the poetic religion of our new worship is not able to accept every manifestation of strong life; for it is as much present in a cancerous bed-chamber as in the freedom and innocence of an Easter cowslip meadow.

How strangely confused are the associations that make up the sequence of our thoughts! The sound of the sheepdog's barking, the sound of this faithful animal "with jagged teeth," brought the vigorous personality of the shepherd to my mind, and this made me recall a Sunday afternoon when I had passed him in Poxwell spinney, walking by the side of a girl with a bunch of yellow irises in his hand. It had interested me to see how passion could awaken an appreciation of beauty in the rudest mind.

The recollection of these flowers now set me pondering upon the tragic love felt by Polyphemus for his sea-nymph, Galatea. For, according to Theocritus, it was these very flowers that he used to be diligent to find for the delight of Galatea when she was still too young to torment him with her aloofness, or torture him with wanton infidelities. The ancient story is a moving one, and to my mind this morning it seemed to bind poetry to poetry, like an anthology for ever fresh down the long centuries. In a marginal dimension that exists always side by side with the market-day world the same frenzy is potent to-day to work its transforming spells, rendering the rough gentle and the monster mild as fawn or song bird. In his time Polyphemus, against all expectation, resolved his trouble through song, through poetry. Many were the evenings, so the antique legend assures us, that his sheep came drifting back through the dew of dusk masterless and unshepherded to the shelter of their hurdled fold, while he, the uncouth victim of the Cyprian's shaft, loitered on by the sea's margin idling after each incoming wave for a glimpse of the maid of his choice. The recollections of soft summer hours when she, who was whiter than whey, had allowed him to play with her; had allowed him to hold her ears in his two hands, better suited though they were for holding a crook; so that he might, as the phrase was, kiss her "by the pot," stirred his lusty Cyclopean blood beyond all sense.

As now, so then, it was the nights that were most difficult to get through. In the long-drawn-out periods of his distracted insomnia Polyphemus would compose his most beautiful poetry. Out of the dark recesses of his historic cave his inspired words would float, till the sea-glens of Sicily would echo and re-echo to his wild madrigals. But she, his only love, sleeping in her sand-strewn water-shadowed cavern, had no care. Though he lamented his single eyebrow "long and arched" she remained untouched; though he reminded her of the "luces" they had found together, he could not win her attention; though he threw to the moon his passionate refrain of what might have been, no mention of his happy sheep, of his cave, of his bed, aromatic with juniper, could break through her indifference. With the passionate intensity of a nightingale in a garden hedge this awkward, one-eyed giant, with terrible rapture, with terrible pain, cast into his tremulous heart-breaking music his living soul. She did not mind, she did not reck of it, she whose wayward fancy had been bewitched by her leman shepherd.

About our dædal planet the same moon moves that once imparted a shadow to the monumental form of this King of all the Cyclops; in our hearts we find the same sweet disorders. Just as Polyphemus pastured his sheep, driving the stakes for his cotes deep into virgin soil, so are sheep pastured to-day; and this very summer, make no doubt of it, in many a chiff-chaff spinney the shy reluctances of lovely girls will be wooed away by the haughty splendour of this common fleur-de-lis!

NATURAL HAPPINESS

SINCE our primitive forefathers first looked about them with conscious thought how many strange notions have got into our heads! We have deceived ourselves in every possible way. No illusion has been too fantastic for our superstitious speculations. It would seem that almost everything visible has at one time or other been an object of worship—stones, trees, animals, birds, fishes; and we have gone so far as to credit the very grasshoppers with similar intentions, as they rest in the hay with brittle knees crooked.

To see the skull of a man cast out of a grave by the spade of a country sexton is a provocative experience. This odd pot of bone, with lost handles, belongs to the only animal who has dared to tease subject-matter with witty innuendoes. All the other beasts of the field have been content with their hour of life, have asked no more than to feel the sun upon their hides, and to devour, and to swallow water. Man alone has been partial to discontent; the slugs even show complacence as, with silent secret perspicacity, they draw towards the undefended seedlings of their appetites.

The number of pernicious misconceptions that have been ready set for our childish minds can never be catalogued. We are all of us the same—black skins, brown skins, yellow skins, and white skins; all of us no better than precocious apes snapping at shadows. We awake out of an infinite oblivion to find ourselves alive on a sturdy planet of miracle and mystery. The myths of antiquity trickily preserved in pot-hook ciphers hedge us in with erroneous conclusions.

How can we be expected to envisage existence with a clear, disinterested intelligence?

We grow up obsessed with the legends of our particular locality. We are dominated by the persuasions of custom. Our kings on their gilded thrones, our dressed-up judges, convince our flighty minds as to the stability of society, and not once in a lifetime do we see behind such administrative expedients. The priest rises to bless us with pontifical fingers punctiliously arranged, and his large claim provokes no protest. We do not see him as a direct representative of sacerdotal Egypt, an obsolete witch-doctor out of the remote past, invoking the aid of beings that never existed except in the bewildered dreams of savages. Meanwhile, on every side the stir of life continues with its weasel wickedness, its may-fly triviality, and its inexplicable inclination towards what is gentle, altruistic, and good.

The cuckoo's hollow echo comes to us through our breakfast window, troubling with its promise both maid and yellow-hosed bachelor. Swift as a half-seen fairy, a mouse crosses the garden path, a diminutive questing beast, the quiver of a lobelia flower the only proof of its passing. The white campion in the hayfield gives out to the June night its sweet breath. With bellies full of the blood and flesh of fellow animals we stand up to practise self-interested pieties, the claws on our fingers carefully disguised with gloves.

Punctually once a day the earth is turned from the sun's disc, and the benison of sleep falls upon all—falls upon the little princess in her palace-bed, falls upon the haymaker with his stiff back, falls upon the unscrupulous midnight fornicator; none being excluded from this recurring respite, from this repeated draught of blessed annihilation. It is a dispensation of widest scope; the horse with its enormous odd-shaped cranium experiences it, the willow wren also, swaying on a pendulous reed, with tiny skull cradled beneath feathers. Then again the sun rises, and from one side of the hemisphere to the other all is clatter. The birds chirp and twitter, the animals disturb yards and fields with rude unintelligent voices, and men continue to deceive themselves with frozen words.

Below this diurnal procession, so trivial, so profound, so paltry, so heroic, the ultimate laws of Nature continue uninterrupted. Obedient to their ordering, the nebulas of the firmament are congregated and dispersed, and fire burns and water drowns; and the Abbot's body, with its wicker-basket ribs, is slowly and inevitably transmuted into dust, be his mediæval stone coffin never so tight.

Even in the few days that are allowed us, days no more in number than could be added together by a child in a nursery, we can observe these disciplined energies at their unending task of destruction and creation. Nothing on this earth has permanence. Knuckle-inch by knuckle-inch the sarsen blocks of Stonehenge are crumbling away, while within the gigantic circle of Avebury there springs up a village scarce mindful of the past. Beyond the famous Gate of Damascus, where generations of camels have knelt for their burdens, where David walked, and Solomon, his hair powdered with gold dust, jested, a government building has now been erected for the use of smart Civil servants. A few years will go by, and all once more will be altered; and these sandstones of sanctity, this crucifixion mould, will be disturbed for some quite new and unforeseen purpose. There is no rock of ages. Where for summers grass grew, there is now wheat, and where the sheep were folded, docks. Between our cradle and our grave time is no longer than a rook boy's whistle, and yet long enough to recognise this process of passing, passing, passing.

We see it, acknowledge it, and yet a moment later the wisest of us is to be found disturbed over affairs that have no substance of constancy in them. Idealists have made wide use of this perpetual flux in their homilies. This fundamental rule of earth-existence has given them many a brave opportunity for pressing home their doctrines of denial. All ends in death. In death all human activity is cancelled. How many men does not one see struck down without reason like forest stags in the pride of their grease? It is death's pastime to play such tricks; there is no jape more common. Men stay idling after legacies, and before a month is past it is they themselves that keep company with coffin beetles. On Lady Day a grocer stands snug before his packages, his gay tins of preserved fruit on the shelf above his head; before Easter the tapes of his apron have been unloosed for his swaddling shroud. There is confusion in this clerkly reasoning. To give oneself over to worldly interests, to social ambitions, nothing is more foolish; but there is no good reason for any indiscriminate disparagement of the pleasures of the senses. All human knowledge, all moralities, all religions, derive ultimately from these messengers. It is out of their twilight whisperings that supernatural heavens have originated. Our haughty minds are nothing but the senses in flower. When the senses wither and die the mind withers and dies with them.

Far from distrusting the temporal delights that come through the body, we should abandon ourselves to them with confidence. The way of the senses is the way of life. It is the people with their hands in the till and their eyes on heaven who ruin existence. There should be open-air temples in every town and village where philosophers could expound this soundest of doctrines. Why is half the population tormented with restraints, obedience to which in no way furthers the public good? Because the priests for generations have been confederate with the money-makers, and they both know very well that if natural happiness were allowed the generations would no longer accept their shrewd worldly maxims, no longer be so docile, so easy to be exploited. Without doubt half the ethical rules they din into our ears are designed to keep us at work.

From the epoch when the human race gave up its free wandering life and began to sow and reap and domesticate animals, false values became popular. Civilised life lays emphasis upon property, upon gold and silver, and oxen and asses; heathen life looks for its rewards from bodily enjoyment. There is no doubt that the acquisitive impulse is especially damaging to human felicity. As soon as it becomes a predominating obsession, evil and misery are everywhere present. War follows war, religious persecution religious persecution; then slavery, exploitation, and deepest woe. With the desire for possessions the very nature of man alters. Merely to be alive should be sufficient reason for happiness. Natural happiness should be the prerogative of men and women, just as it is the prerogative of the mole in its winding tunnel or the stickleback in its shining stream. I learned this from watching the natives in Africa. When uninterfered with by the white settlers they command this passage-way to natural happiness. They work for amusement, and never for drudgery. They find sufficient reward in being about under the sun, content with water and scant victuals. Though this folk are as black as devils, I never saw one of them with an expression mean or ill-tempered. Unperverted by sordid interests, they have retained their spiritual health, and are superior to us in their attitude as are butterflies to pismires.

Nothing is more lamentable than to see the number of lives sacrificed, utterly wasted, in the Western world to-day—each worker with his own petty preoccupation walking forward to the grave as though drugged. Our education is directed towards this end. We must learn how to be successful; he whose coffers are most full is most highly extolled. Education worthy of the name should have but one purpose—to teach us how to live the fullest possible lives in whatever state it should have pleased God to call us, whether in a counting-house, or in the common market-place, or in a gaol. Always we should be taught to be conscious and more conscious, to be accessible to ideas, to be receptive to sense impressions. We should be taught to be expert in love-making. We should come from our schools fortified against mischance, knowing that nothing matters as long as we remain healthy and alive.

Too many men and women spend their time between an office and a home in a state of intellectual stupor. No human being should ever wake without looking at the sun with grateful recognition of the liberty of another day; nor give himself to sleep without casting his mind, like a merlin, into the gulfs between the furthest stars. We are all of us grossly constituted. To listen for a moment to the wind as it stirs the leaves of our garden trees, and to realise that this murmur was troubling earth vegetation before men were, and will be troubling it when they have gone, is to take knowledge of the breath of the infinite. It is a mystery, a sign for everyone, this movement of the planet's atmosphere. It dislodges the dust in the belfry where the owl stares and a loose board rattles. The nettles grouped by the farmyard wall sway to it, and in wide open spaces its music is not lost. No message comes through our senses but is full of worship—the taste of brown bread and red wine, the smell of a field of dazzling charlock, the sight of swallows sweeping back and forth over the tilted roof of a barn, the cool fair flesh of a young girl's body, the liquid song of a blackbird in the white twilight of the longest day. The Cretans used to assert that the grave of Jupiter was in their locality. They knew the place well, and would often play tipcat there, or weave insect cages for their children out of the sweet vernal grasses that grow so plentifully where earth has been newly disturbed. When, in the autumn weather of last year, I passed a mangel grave in the corner of a certain field I could not help fancying it to be the sepulchre of my father's God, and that if I had had the temerity to remove the straw and to lift the heavy sods, something else than roots, round and golden, would have been revealed! We are projected down the tunnels of our individual fates like peas along hollow fennel stalks, and except for an occasional and unaccountable windfall-fling from the hands of that wanton, Chance, there is no meddling with our ordered flight. The village atheist's reasoning has always been sound. If we moved and had our being under the eyes of an omnipotent Creator, then he would be indolent and callous beyond pardon. Every day it is possible to see happenings sufficiently stupid and cruel to estrange all sensitive spirits.

Let us pass over such foibles. The human predicament remains the same. We can do nothing better than to fling our bodies and souls before the god of life, passionately and without reserves, as oblations of golden wine are thrown from a cup. By acknowledging the value of tenderness we shall grow wise enough to check the too exorbitant demands of our gluttonous desires, while at the same time we can still be at liberty to treasure every hour of our days, recreant never to the ancient atheistical mystery of existence, our hearts full of worship, as are the tares of our garden, for the only tutelary influence that sways our planet, the life-giving Sun.

UNICORN LEGENDS

In these days, when men of science declare that the physical laws governing the universe are not as fixed as was supposed, our belief that true religion should consist in the contemplation of the poetry of existence is more than ever justified. With the utmost alacrity orthodox theologians have appropriated for their own superstitious turn these opportune gaps in the scientific summary. With this arrant reasoning in mind, we need no longer be concerned to defend traditional imaginings; for surely the tree of life in our sense-apprehended world does draw its sap from deep-set Ygdrasil roots.

In what then does our natural faith consist? In a heightened awareness of the stream of earth-life as it moves past in our moment of space-time. It is a faith that obstinately repudiates all dogmas, and believes that consciousness is its own justification. This spontaneous persuasion rests upon a sensitive sense of earth-existence as it is revealed to each generation from the day of birth to the day of death. Early man held to this simple metaphysic when he stood in speechless awe before each unexpected manifestation of the natural world, before the glittering transformation of geometric frost marks, before the thunder of the heavens. Modern man holds to it whenever with a free mind he realises the utter isolation of his soul.

In such a state the most fanciful legends have for him a significant message. Consider, for example, the ancient rumour of the unicorn. It is of no consequence to him whether the fabulous creature ever "really and truly" lived. There may never have been unicorns "milk-white all over except nose, mouth, nostrils"; or, as Sir Thomas Browne made bold to suggest, there may have been "many kinds thereof." It does not matter. To such an earth-born one it is sufficient that so strange, so lovely a conception should ever have got into man's head at all, should have got into it and continued to bewilder it with delight for so many succeeding centuries. His preoccupation is always with this lyrical, with this ballad quality that celebrates human history, this romance that, as it were, with the sound of flutes, attends every delusion that has ever been entertained by a human being born upon this lost earth, upon this earth washed by salt seas, adorned with grasses, ornamented with fluttering birds. It suffices for such a worshipper that our churchyards are sown thick with the skulls of men who believed in the existence of the unicorn.

It has been suggested that the tale owed its origin, and its power over men's imaginations, to a half-conscious, sublimated, ithyphallic association; and this assumption would seem to explain what is taught about the intimate comportment of the stately, aristocratic animal. The legend of the unicorn can be taken as an almost perfect example for illustrating the irrelevance of everyday facts, of everyday truths, to anyone whose deepest experience rests upon the spirit rather than upon the letter. It would be impossible to over-treasure this ancient hearsay as an imaginative contribution to the wild history of man.

The religion of poetry rests to-day, as it did in the time of Homer, on an impassioned appreciation of appearances. It is an austere religion that demands a certain detachment, a certain selfless dedication. When once, however, we have become initiates, how rich is our reward! Never again, not for a single moment, can we become submerged by the importunities of unillumined reality; the least favourable daily incident finding a place in our particular poetic perspective, in this inspired perspective that never loses sight of our lot upon this planet, a planet dancing in sunlit space, inhabited by animals grown wise; by a breed of dreamers malign and magnanimous, sturdily camped in their generations upon a corn-bearing tilth, and covetous of an unending spirit life.

The ancient lore that surrounds the unicorn story is redolent of the fairy-like invention of earth's phantom populations. It is no clodhopper record. This beast "with armour on its brow" is conceived proudly enough. He is a high-spirited animal that loves solitude and frequents undisturbed waste lands. God Almighty, exulting over His handiwork, selects the unicorn, the *re'em*, to flout Job with. "Will the unicorn be willing to serve thee, or abide by thy crib? . . . Canst thou bind the unicorn with his band in the furrow? Or will he harrow the valleys after thee?" Always the unicorn is represented as a mettlesome creature, a quadruped of hot humours, only to be captured, so the ancients delivered, through its "property" of sexual susceptibility. If a true virgin sat alone in a flowery mead, then this high beast would come out of the forest to lay its beautiful *blanche* head upon her lap, and while it remained thus, besotted by the girl's caresses, the hunters would be able to approach it, to catch it, to kill it. It was out of this older story that the idea of the Holy Hunt arose, with Jesus symbolised by the sacrificed unicorn.

Fancies upon fancies, imaginings upon imaginings, illusions upon illusions; and yet how charged, how penetrated beyond all expectations with the wonder, the miracle of our earth's nursery rhyme. What a high victory is here for man's mind. Think of him arising from his brutish estate of clubs and fist-flints, hairy, muscular, mud-begotten; and presently, in no time at all, passing on from one immovable flap ear to another immovable flap ear of his rude fellows this entranced, moon-impregnated story.

It is nothing to us whether such tales be false or true in the ordinary sense of those slippery words. It does not matter whether Christ lived or did not live. The important thing is that His personality, so simple to some, so complicated to others, so pathetic, so tragic, was ever projected out of man's abused heart. These unicorn stories are illuminated scraps torn from God's scroll—for what is truth? Nothing more sure than an inspired momentary glimpse of eternity vouchsafed to mortals between birth and dusty death.

A GRAVE IN DORSET

BEFORE us in the noonday rose the great headlands of the Dorset coast, Bats Head, Swyre Head, Hambury Tout, lying one behind the other, to where the upland lawns of St. Aldhelm's Head stretch out into the Channel. As far as eye could scan no movement was visible on the flanks of the wide downs. Unresponsive, unmoved, their gorse-covered slopes confronted our anxious eyes. We climbed each of the great hills broken into clear chalk cliffs against the sea. From an altitude of five hundred feet we traced the long curves of the deserted beaches below, and then, in what seemed but a moment of time, we were ourselves moving over those bright sea-banks. Under the smugglers' chain we discovered footprints. It was high tide. Could it be that during the interval that had passed since he entered the sea the encroaching water had carried away his clothes? Back we went. By the time we had reached the second burial mound the sun was sinking towards Hardy's monument in the west. Already the cormorants were flying round the White Nose to their nesting-places. With weary tread we made our way to Harry Miller the fisherman, who lives two miles westward from the White Nose, and asked him to row his boat along under the cliffs. We watched the small craft till it was out of sight, but two hours later it had returned. Nothing had been seen.

Surely, we thought, he might even yet come back. We entered his room. All his scant worldly possessions remained in their places in the same meticulous order in which he had left them. It was the end of the month of May, and at that time of the year the glow of twilight is so soon replaced by the first wanness of dawn that the small hours of our watch, with the door of our kitchen left ajar, were soon over. Once again we were out on the headlands overlooking a sea white and colourless as a hempen shroud. In the stillness of that hour there appeared against some protruding chalk rocks two animals following one behind the other—badgers returning to their earth! No sight could have brought better to our tormented minds the indifference of the natural world to our trouble. On all sides there was taking place unarrested the engendering of new life. Doe-rabbits in darkened tunnels were bringing to birth, were nurturing their blind and naked offspring; in snug "forms" hares were suckling their leverets; the young ravens in their nest on the Durdle Door were calling to their dark mother for meat. Already the peregrine falcon had killed its prey, already the adder had slid from its retreat to where the sun could warm its compact scales.

Again we watched the fisherman navigating his boat over the water. He approached the West Bottom and disappeared behind the Fountain Rock. We waited. The reappearance of the boat seemed delayed beyond all reason. I knew the sea pool where the boat was. In the storms of winter no place along the coast was capable of presenting an aspect more formidable. At such a time it seemed forgotten, abandoned to the sea's desolate fury. In summer weather it is different. It is here that the guillemots gather to nest, becking at each other or fluttering out to sea in circles, to return with legs astraddle to their stained platforms.

Once more the boat appeared. Far distant as I was, the dead head of our friend was clearly visible. We hurried down the precipitous path to where we knew the boat could come to shore. This then was the hearse of Walter Franzen, this his carriage of death. The broad oars creaked in their rowlocks; the unbailed water at the bottom of the boat washed to and fro with the gentle heaving of the sea, and there in the stern he lay, a steersman who had no care for the tiller. Though he had fallen from the top of the cliff his body appeared unhurt. His lips still wore their expression of unoffending pride. His grey flannel trousers were torn as those of a boy's might be torn who had fallen on a hard road. Through the rent a white knee-cap protruded, familiar and reassuring in shape and appearance. We touched his hand, that hand whose aristocratic fingers were trailing in the water. Was this the hand, this unliving hand from which all blood had been withdrawn, that had broken bread, cast stones, wielded axes, and caressed the soft cheeks of those sad, bereft ones who had so loved him? Could he not speak to us, tell us what had happened, blame his slippery shoes, explain that he was only looking over when a boulder gave way hurtling him to a violent death? Alas, never again would we hear his protesting laugh, never again be taught gentleness by his unassuming ways.

As we climbed back up the path, all that had happened during the past few hours came to our memory; we recalled the sensitive, almost guilty look he had worn when we surprised him suddenly outside Judge Jeffreys' house in Dorchester and he thought he had kept us waiting; remembered the consideration he had shown, his reserve, his solitary humour. "I have three hours," he had said on starting out towards the sea. His watch was stopped at a quarter to one o'clock, and from where he fell he was exactly fifteen minutes from our cottage on the White Nose. He fell a little to the east of the Fountain Rock. What a monument Fate has prepared for him! Here indeed was a cenotaph, we thought, as we stood by the side of that mighty bastion ribbed with flint. If his neck had to be broken, this place was well selected; better that it should happen here in one single moment of desperate consciousness, where the herring gulls never cease from crying, better in such a place than in the gambling dens of New York, for there was not one of us, not one of his friends or lovers, who did not feel assured in their hearts that his disdain of life would bring him to no old man's grave.

It is not often that I entertain a priest in my house, but as chance would have it now my cousin from Boston stood knocking as the body was carried through our garden gate. He brought with him what consolation the ancient pieties could give. With lips that could utter no word, the young man lay before us uncommunicating, august. I tried to stamp for ever upon my mind the beauty of that fallen head.

Three days later we followed the farm wagon which carried his coffin to the churchyard of East Chaldon. Along grassy tracks by the edge of cornfields and through wide, silent valleys, where the horse's hoofs were muffled by the soft turf, our way lay. The weather was still fine. The sun splashed down upon the shadowless slopes and upon the field of mustard that bordered the lane. Immediately before me there trod an aged labourer in a coat black as the feathered back of a crow. With a smell of dusty horse-dung rising from the road I looked at the neck of this old man, so deeply wrinkled with "noughts and crosses" wrinkles, and thought of his father and his father's father, who had all probably worn this same black braided garment on a hundred such occasions. Wherever a man lives there also is sorrow. I continued to follow the elm-wood coffin almost hidden under its burden of blue-bells, buttercups, pink campions, and branches of May blossom.

Up the path and into the church we carried him, into that village church which still contains within its walls a font cut out of a massive block of stone by Saxon masons more than a thousand years ago. In such a place the words of the poet could not fall on the ears of the congregation without understanding. "For a thousand years in thy sight are but as yesterday; seeing that it is past as a watch in the night. Thou turnest man to destruction; again thou sayest, Come again, ye children of men. As soon as thou scatterest them, they are even as a sleep; and fade away suddenly like the grass."

GOD

WITH Teutonic bluntness Feuerbach long ago asserted, "There is no God, it is clear as the sun and as evident as the day that there is no God. . . ." If we are to believe the *New English Dictionary*, the origin of the taunting word with which he is concerned may be found in two Aryan roots, one of which suggested invocation and the other the act of pouring out, as in a libation. The word seems to have come into general use after the last Ice Age, when a scantling of nomadic herdsmen, by means of the domestication of wild animals, initiated a rudimentary society. Relieved from the exigencies incident to the pressing economies of the huntsman and berry-eater, their untutored minds found leisure to invent this ambiguous etymon, the cause of so much vexation to the thought of their descendants.

The notions associated with this root word, Gheu, have been, if I may venture to say so, "a little on the exacting side." In the hope of rendering our prayers more acceptable we have been at pains to offer sacrifices, either in the form of material possessions, or in the form of moral restraints, refraining from doing just those very things that we most want to do; the power reputed to lurk behind this arrangement of letters being assumed to be as susceptible to crude propitiations as are human beings. Unfortunately, after twenty thousand years it seems more than probable that all our sacrifices have been endured in vain, the hypothesis of the deity's existence being to-day as uncertain as at the beginning. The fact is that the scales of this particular metaphysical balance are so nicely adjusted that the seed of an Abyssinian coral flower would be of sufficient weight to tilt them either way. We might as well try to snatch at a ghost as to try to understand God. Those who support established customs, having an eye to the welfare of their souls, their skins, and their pockets, hold tenaciously to the "larger hope," while the rest of us raggle-taggle gypsies are unable to forget the thirty-nine sulky articles that go to show that this odd word is but a symbol for a disconcerting void.

I myself have always felt the greatest sympathy for the point of view of that astronomer who spent a lifetime in scrutinising the night sky with his telescope in order, if possible, to see God with his own eyes. It is reported that on one very clear night, when it was so frosty that the poor hedge birds were starving, as he was scanning a little carelessly one of those darker areas of the milky way, which Herschel used to call "holes in the sky", something suddenly did swim into his ken, not dissimilar to the eye of a peacock, to the eye of a very bright, peering, princely peacock, a trifle unsympathetic! The sky area in which it appeared was near the constellation of Scorpio, that is to say at the very centre point about which our particular star-stream is said to be rotating. In the excitement that the practical philosopher felt at finding this mysterious bird-scorpion's eye at the very heart of our island universe, he foolishly began to readjust his lenses so as to obtain a still clearer view, but alas, when he had turned the wheel, which happened to work a bit stiffly, the eye had vanished, and as he stepped to the window of his watch-tower, duster still in hand, all he could see were the same constellations with which we are familiar, the same silent stars, cold and undistracted, eternal and sublime.

This telescopic glimpse and the backside perspective view that Moses was favoured with from his rocky cleft upon

Mount Sinai, are, if I am not mistaken, the only recorded occasions when the unknown quantity behind the Aryan word has ever been seen by mortals. I mean seen with the homely certainty of the human senses, as a modest ass might be seen, standing patiently in the centre of a hot and thirsty market-place.

There is without doubt something enervating in taking so thin a conjecture too seriously. There is nothing in nature to justify a scientific inference for the existence of the God of our infantile conception. If men could once get it clearly into their heads that the affairs of the earth depend entirely upon their own efforts and that the last hope of outside intervention must be abandoned, our situation would be on the way to improvement. Sustained by an ever-present consciousness of our freedom, so efficient a reorganisation of the world's commonwealth would take place that in no time there would be wool caps for all, wine for all, bread for all and girls for all.

Let us once more contemplate our predicament. We are, Chinese, white men, negroes, marooned together on a disorderly and disastrous planet, the belly of which at any moment may begin to belch out fire, a planet which retains the semblance of steadiness, as, like a *dragon volans*, it sweeps forward resistless and buoyant about the Sun. Alone, alone, alone, a race of animals, accidentally equipped with frivolous brains, enmeshed in the carnate snare of their brute beast origin, and yet with their hearts stirred, like a gaggle of migrating geese, by an unutterable insistent longing. Men and women, these bounding apes that must every day void dross, by a sweepstake chance have won divine thought, thought potent to destroy, potent to save. On the earth and in the unthinkable regions around the earth ordered adjustments, out of the reach of perceptive understanding, are for ever taking place. This magnetic fabric, volatile and at the same time determined, is the cat's cradle of life, is reality. God is the unspiritual shiver of matter that is and was and will be for ever. This subatomic phenomenon exists, together with the phantoms of flesh it casts up, whether observed by the human mind or not, a sempiternal absolute as efficient to expand an island universe as to project into a flash of space-time the delicate ithyphallus of a chalk-hill-blue embracing its painted darling upon a stalk of grass on Wednesday morning. The wind roaming in obedience about our chimney-pots of baked clay is God; the lava boiling in the mouth of a crater is God; the massed water of the sea subsiding into waves of enormous weight is God.

Yesterday I was awake early and watched the dawn come up across the cold fields. The light spread itself over the downs with impatience. First the hedges became visible, then small birds passed by me in dusky succession, then I saw a rat with hairless tail returning to its hole. Far away over their roosting ledges the hungry gulls were audibly clamouring for their meat. During those timeless moments I saw the earth with its creature life unmindful of the fretful presence of man. It was suddenly apparent, beyond all dispute, that the whole human riot, with its religions, its political cozenage, its compassion, was without any kind of transcendental surveillance, without any kind of significance other than the passionate worship, carnal and poetic, of the glory of life.

A MOON CIRCUS

FROM the actors who draw from us laughter and tears on the
theatre stages of our great cities down to the meanest
mountebank acrobat at a country fair, how commendable in
every way are the entertainers of the human race! These
tumblers, in whatever form they appear, are God's children.
They are the cuckoos of our kind, and in their migrations are
never tired of calling upon us to be merry. Whenever I see
even a Punch and Judy I envy the showman his pastime.
These strolling players earn their bread in no sour way as is
the lot of so many of the rest of us. Their packs may be
rough and hard, but they lie lightly on their shoulders.
They let the world wag as it will; it is none of their business.
If with long-jointed straws they can tickle our chins, that is
sufficient.

It was with a feeling of the keenest satisfaction that I
entered the small square of Belley the other afternoon to see
that a band of French gypsies had come to town with their
circus. And the delight I felt at the first sight I caught of the
gaily-coloured vans was fully justified. Belley is a small
mountain city in the Bugey on the borders of Savoy. It is
seldom enough that any amusement is offered to its
inhabitants, and the open space was already alive with
eager onlookers. For these wine-tasters, for all their hard
work in the upland vineyards, have a natural relish for
mummery. The little troupe was busy preparing for the
evening, and when I returned at nine o'clock all was in order.
The circus ring, made of circular boards over which you

could step, was illumined by a tall maypole strung with two or three lights. Also, as it happened, a full moon rose that evening above the jagged mountains, the *Dents du Chat*, to help them in their play. Dangling from the maypole by a crossbar and a network of ropes was the trapeze upon which the acrobats were to perform. Nothing could have been more elementary. The sharp, flinty stones of the square with the charmed circle—the goblin's circle—were covered with a sprinkling of sawdust to make the ground less slippery for the performing horses. At one end of the circle was the grand stand, an erection of rickety, narrow boards constructed in four tiers.

I took my place in good time, but I need not have done so, for not one of the crowd could the gypsies persuade to approach those formal seats. Again and again they stood under the maypole and harangued them. "Here are the seats prepared for you, my good sirs, won't you be seated? It is no wisdom to stand all through a summer evening. Two francs is the cost. Would you grudge us two francs? What is this that we do? We have to eat to live like you. Our horses must have corn and we bread to put in our mouths. By God, if you will not be seated like a sensible audience, the devil of any circus shall you see. We will drive away under this bright moon."

To all these expostulations the crowd gave small heed, but continued standing about, content with the knowledge that on their own feet they would be in a position to see as well as any. These rustics, with bullock's dung on their *sabots*, are not easily to be cajoled to part with a franc when a sou will take its place. After each prolation the dark men would retreat to the entrance of the ring, where, with trumpets, drums, and cymbals, they would beat out their jocund music as if they had forgotten the grudge they bore these obstinate grape-gatherers whom again they would be expostulating with to little purpose. I observed them with the greatest sympathy. There was an old man, ragged and bearded, who kept pounding a great drum that he held between his knees. There was a woman, tough and hard and stained with walnut-juice, clapping a pair of cymbals, one against the other. A young man in the prime of life was blowing upon a brazen trumpet. There was a clown, and there were two small boys with painted faces in motley who looked as hungry as any two children I have ever seen. Indeed, this gypsy company was as pathetic as was their little wooden circus circle, two feet high, fit for dwarfs to play leap-frog in.

The entertainment opened. An old white stallion ambled slowly round while the elder of the two boys jumped up at intervals upon his hollow back. Twice, as the horse took the impact his hoofs slipped and he all but fell. A goat now appeared and climbed on to a table, and from there on to a chair, and on to a stool on the chair. In this exalted position, like a chamois on the pinnacle of a miniature Alp, he raised his left leg very gravely. I looked about. The crowd was spellbound, agape with wonder. Every window in every house on the square was open, with all the inmates looking at this singular animal, who, in spite of her heavy udders, the udders that doubtless supplied her master with milk, had so lively a sense of balance. Fortunate indeed, I thought, are the inhabitants of these houses who, from their snug, lighted interiors are able on a fine September night to look down upon a magic circle with a tufted nanny-goat pointing a mystical indicative hoof at the moon.

The clown's "turn" was perhaps best suited to the taste of the populace. This honest fellow, with straw-coloured hair, feigned a toothache. "*Ah, ma mère*," he kept repeating, "*Ah, ma mère*," as he trotted aimlessly round the ring. "What is the matter with you, Brother?" cursed the ringmaster. "*Ah, que je souffre, je souffre. J'ai mal aux dents.* Had the devil ever to suffer so much pain!" To the clown's utmost dismay a dentist was summoned forthwith. He appeared in the form of the smallest of the children, with an enormous pair of pincers. This implement was judged insufficient and a long cord was produced. The clown, now shivering with simulated fright, was seated on a chair in the centre of the ring. It was suggested that he should take off his coat. He did so and lo! underneath was a second; he took this off, but there was still a third. Seven coats he discarded amid shouts of uproarious merriment from the crowd. Not only had he coats in multiple, but hats also; and it was not until these had been removed that an enormous tooth was extracted, large as the molar I once knocked out of the rotting skull of an African rhinoceros. With a howl of pain and astonishment the patient fell over backwards.

The smallest boy was the "star" of the company. Whenever things were getting dull, this suckling, "with his mother's milk scarce dry on his lips," would utter his gags—hopping, skipping, tumbling, grinning—and yet, how pitiable his malapert little face looked in that white light!

There was now an interval in which the crowd was invited to inspect the wild animals, "ferocious beasts of the jungle." I left my seat, and paying an extra franc, entered a small enclosure surrounded by the gypsy vans. Here an old showman, like an evil gaoler, with a flaming acetylene lamp in his hand, uncovered, one after the other, the rough cages. His collection, except for a small, black bear, consisted of monkeys. In one cage he displayed a coloured mandrill from Madagascar, one of those brilliant monstrosities from far-off jungles that to Western eyes appear like nightmare evocations, as though the sure precision of God's genius had suddenly been replaced by the mocking handiwork of a knavish artist. With its ridged nose of bright blue, with its muzzle of brightest scarlet, the fabulous creature gazed out at the congregation of acquisitive peasants with eyes dark and withdrawn and blinking. Its habitation was an old box with iron bands nailed across the front, and it sat there nursing its melancholy, that melancholy which ever possesses the souls of these witless half-brothers of mankind who can only be distracted by spending long, feckless hours in shining forest trees following the dictates of their untutored natures, amid the screams and shrieks and swift, unreasoned activities of their confederates. The irresponsible cruelty of this imprisonment shocked me. It was mediæval in its thoughtlessness, as was the stupid wonder of the Belley crowd. "See, Ladies and Gentlemen, here indeed is a red-snouted devil, observe his teeth well—eh? What a gullet!" The coloured monkey, big and heavy as a baboon, continued to contemplate from his foul dungeon the flaming light that made visible in so garish a manner the physiognomies of the uncouth and crafty beings who had disturbed his dark repose. As he sat thus crouched on his nest of straw, like a manacled maniac in a bedlam locker, it was impossible not to be arrested by his large sad eyes, eyes in colour and expression exactly opposite to what one would have looked to find in so bizarre and outlandish a head. For this popinjay grotesque had beautiful eyes, eyes that were as soft and brown and religious as were the eyes of my own mother.

Out we trooped through an aperture in the flapping sail-cloth and back again to the ring. The little boy, dancing like an imp, kept our attention alive with a hundred unanticipated buffooneries. Presently a chestnut pony was led into the circle. He was a "wise" pony and could count and answer questions by tapping the ground with one of his hoofs and shaking or nodding his head. "Who finds it most difficult to put the cork in a bottle of wine?" he was asked, and immediately the sagacious beast advanced towards one of the standing spectators, a man whose open countenance showed him to be a good cricket on the hearth in any tavern. This sly venture provoked a roar of applause. "Who is for ever fooling with the girls?" and again the pony chose with discrimination. "You are a wise one," said the old man. "Now tell us, my pretty mare, what do you want—corn?" The pony shook her head, ringing her necklace of small brass bells. "Is it hay you have in mind?" "No," responded the animal with the same negative gesture. "Is it applause?" The pony nodded emphatically amid shouts of admiration.

Now the time came for the last and most exciting "act." The man acrobat announced his intention of turning a somersault over the backs of all his animals. A rough spring-board was brought into the ring. The stallion once more made his appearance and took his place next the spring-board; flanking him was the wise mare, and beyond her a roan gelding with his shoulders sadly galled by the loads he had pulled; on the other side of this work-worn nag stood the nanny-goat. From where I sat I could count the ribs of the stallion. Every time he breathed these rounded, bow-shaped bones showed distinct from each other. Surely he presented a moving spectacle, this valiant old begetter of show ponies. His years were heavy upon him. His head drooped and there were deep sagging holes over his eyes that plainly told of his great age. Yet even so his proximity to the "wise" mare did not leave him unresponsive. He raised his distended nostrils, snuffing the wind, nor were there lacking other signs to prove that his spirit was not dead. A burst of laughter from the boors about me greeted his demonstrations. I could feel no disposition towards hilarity. This animal, senile and yet still of so gallant a mettle, offered as he stood there an illustration only too concordant with our own sorrowful betrayal. It was apparent that his triumphs were fast drawing to their inevitable end. Soon enough he would be found with his legs horribly erect among the nettles of a wayside ditch; soon, only too soon, would a fine, green moss be growing in the skull sockets already but scantily covered by his grey hide. It is the way we must all go. It is the way of all flesh. We all of us are given some opportunities of grazing on cow-parsley, cooled and freshened by sweet mountain showers. We all of us are permitted to parade just so many times round our circle, and then, whether the dust under our feet is of gold, of ashes, or of sawdust, our hour strikes. The scaramouch crossed himself like a good Catholic and bounding into the air went whirling over his assembled livestock with the velocity of a hoop. He landed on his feet. "Tell me what is the difference between me and the full moon?" bawled the urchin—"I am full every day and she is full but once a month." I was already half across the square when his words reached my ears and I paused for a moment to imprint the scene once again on my memory. The moon was now high up over the mountains. With its light it charmed the sloping roofs of the ancient town, it edged with silver the wooden shutters, it illumined large patches of the roadway with a brightness almost of noon-time; and as I returned through the vineyards to my cottage I saw the wreathed mists of the water meadows in the valley transformed into motionless gossamer-like clouds. "She is full once a month," I thought, "and it is under her glimpses that we also, in *our* Square of Belley, laugh and cross ourselves and make love and die. And with how little difference! Life itself is but a many-coloured circus developing from sock to sock under the surveillance of the moon, and whether our heels be feathered or leaden it is to the cold grave that they carry us. 'Ripeness is all.'"

WHEN THE UNICORN "CONS" THE WATERS

I HAVE often been told by a man whose spirit I honour, that it is best to pray before dawn and after sunset. At these tremulous hours the massive influence of the triumphant sun is held in abeyance and the awful darkness of the night is not. It was explained to me that this is a secret well known to those versed in the occult lore of human piety, a secret understood by the religious of many nations, and one by no means unrecognised by the wisdom of Rome.

It is certain that in those moods, when the clutch of unredeemed matter is less heavy upon us, and when it almost seems plausible that the mysterious atomic quiver of the objective universe may be, in actual fact, porous to impossible spiritual influences, there can suddenly descend on even the most froward head the echo of strange rumours. This secret lonely echo of a ghostly reality behind the insistent reality that we know so well will suddenly possess us without reason. It can be provoked by the most simple sounds and sights, or even by a common earth-bound odour—the murmur of a bee in a little back garden, the gleam of a wet white pebble upon the margin of the sea, the health-giving smell of a horse's curved neck hot in the sun. Often it is the most inconsiderable message brought by our naughty senses that will set our psychic nerves agog in this unexplained way, agog and yearning for the mystery that lies at the core of life. It is possible, of course, that this mood is but a deception, for no one can live for half a century without having learned to regard with suspicion those intimations that the senses are so prompt to present to the artless consciousness of our adventuring souls.

These whispers are received each year by the young and by the old. For months they are not there, and then they are suddenly and utterly present like children coming in through a garden gate with spring flowers in their hands. It may be that they will be carried to us with the sound of the Lulworth bells, fitfully heard at Christmas time over the bare thorn hedges of the downs; or it may be when we listen to the first cock blackbird's song rising clear from an allotment hedge, when the plot is still only "roughed up," and the broad beans have not yet been sown. On such occasions, for a moment instant as the leap of a spotted trout, swift as the flash of a kingfisher, we feel convinced that only an inch beyond our mortal ken a fairy kingdom does actually exist.

Many minds are naturally obstinate and disinclined to be taken in by pleasant and fanciful dreams, and I find my own to be of such a temper. Yet there are occasions when even the most grudging child of the irreligious sun cannot help pouring out admiration from his delighted soul for the mere chance of finding himself alive upon a planet as strange and unpredictable and exciting as ours. It is at such moments of innocent transport that we should pray before sunrise and after sunset, pray prayers that have for their purpose no personal advantage, but are as native as are the vesper cries of pairing partridges, and as full of natural gratitude as is the heart of a lover. It is the stupidity of our minds that prevents us from seeing existence as a mystery wilder than the dream of Devil or God. We stand before the throne of life sullen and dull. So blunt is the apprehension of most of us that we are content to spend our priceless and peculiar hours in a state of anæsthesia put upon us by a fatal herd hypnotism.

Oh for a conversion, for a revelation to break up for ever our trivial visions!

Before us are the silver sands and beyond them the waves of Weymouth Bay, shimmering like the bright path of Aphrodite, and yet we remain uncognisant of our chance privilege as children of men in an unreturning hour come down to the shore of the ancient sea to run, to dance, and to laugh with happiness.

You are alive. Millions and millions of your kind who have lived upon earth are now dead. Millions and millions who will live upon the earth will be dead; and yet any old man dozing in the sun is at this instant relishing his dot of time out of eternity. With any mother watching her children at play it is the same; and it is the same with a boy and girl, their thoughts, their bodies shivering under the glamour of their passion.

We are every day betrayed by the blank stare of custom. The commonplace accessories of commonplace people weigh us down. We accept life on its surface value. The Jubilee clock, a newspaper fluttering against a beach chair, a banana skin half buried in the sand—to an enlightened mind even such objects of actuality can be compelled to render up their poetic essences. The Jubilee clock, so expert an example of its complacent period, is tracing out now, very now, upon its bland white face your own apportioned interval of gladness and sorrow. The tattered news-sheet, for all its depressing ordinary look, is composed of an adroit web of fibrous matter from the forest trees of far Labrador. The skin of this fruit was of this very shape and texture when Babylon was being built. Look with your living eyes at the long line of white cliffs, rising and falling, falling and rising. towards St. Aldhelm's Head. How fair and strong a bulwark they make, like a white rampart wall of the earth's end: yet before ever White Nose, Swyre Head, Bats Head, and Rings Hill had risen out of the sea's floor (for the substance that makes up the Dorset downs is nothing but crushed sea-shells) muscular outlandish monsters of saurian shape were feeding, and splashing in lukewarm lagoons only a few miles from where you now are.

All that long epoch has been swallowed up by time. We are here. We are gone. We are here. We are gone.

In ancient days it is reported that the unicorn alone of all the beasts of the field had the power of drawing evil humours out of water. It was said to "con" the waters when it did this, and it did it by touching the surface of the water with its horn. When the forest animals—wild boars, deer, hares, stoats, hedgehogs, badgers—came to drink they would patiently wait the arrival of this fabulous creature in order, so it was said, that they might have the advantage of drinking when pools and fountains of their choice would be free of poison. The unicorn could best perform this miracle at the hour after sunset and at the hour before dawn. It is at the same twilights that human beings can draw nearest to the heart of existence. It is then that they can best give expression to their secret yearnings. It is perhaps then, and then alone, that the miracle of life can become suddenly apparent, apparent in the growth of a dry, salty plant of thrift on a cliff's ledge, apparent in the tiny curled heap of a sand-worm near to a child's spade and bucket.

We must not, however, grow too despondent if for hours, if for days, if for months, we remain engrossed like beasts of burden in the illusion of our humdrum activities. Man is an animal given over to folly as well as to dreams. Sooner or later these heaven-sent moments will be again with us. The forehead horn of the great white beautiful animal will have touched the water, a halcyon calm will be upon the bay, and our outcast prayers of life-gratitude will rise again from seashore sands, from bright buttercup meadows, from silent and familiar rooms, as easily, as naturally, as freely as birds on their migratory flights.

A LOCUST MESSAGE

DURING those periods when we are weighed down by the concerns of everyday life, when it seems that moments of inspiration, of philosophic insight, will never come again, it is often a good thing to rouse our sloth by particular methods of thinking. Yesterday I was resting on the cliffs of Dorset when suddenly an aeroplane, brittle and glittering as a locust, came pressing across the sky with direct humming advance. I resented its intrusion, resented the presence of one of these precise machines that always suggest so saucy an invasion of the blameless heavens. As a matter of fact, its appearance led my imprisoned mind to its way of escape.

I began to fancy that it carried some alien intelligence from the far margins of the universe come to inspect our planet. I saw this visitor draw nearer and nearer, and shared the immediate impressions flashed in upon him, saw the sparkle of the sunshine on the sea, happiest of all earth sights, saw the dazzling whiteness of the chalk headlands, saw the massed green hue of the solid corn-fields behind! And then the gulls came into view, God's very doves rising from their dizzy cotes, and moth-like guillemots, with stiff fluttering wings, making a succession of flights from their ledges to the waves; and beyond, on the firm hills, sweating in the summer heat, two confederate animals, the larger on four legs, the smaller on two legs, moving, one behind the other, with the weary concentration of a laborious purpose. A more exact observation would reveal other unanticipated phenomena: the sea, under its shimmering surface, affording pasture ground for the strangest creatures; for creatures with self-absorbed gibbous eyes, which, without wings or legs, are for ever glancing backwards and forwards through the shining element. Indeed, there would be no end to the supreme wonders—the gripping, awry crabs under the rocks, the landweeds, with their modest presentations, the sea-weeds in all their fern-like slippery beauty!

He would see sufficient miracle on this planet of life-giving, love-engendering dust to convert the most frozen intelligence ever tutored in sidereal mathematics. What more amazing than that the sable wing of a bat, the jewel-bright fin of a mackerel, the rusty red housing jacket of a fox should have taken their present forms? Made from what? From inert clay, from quivering atoms? Consider the insects marshalled into their inch-deep territory under the turf, diminutive serpents of frightful design fitted with a hundred legs, preoccupied presbyterian beetles, the civil ants with their hanging galleries of sieved mould, and everywhere, unassuming, unobtrusive, the all-conquering laily worm!

Life freely scattered in every direction over the earth's surface, life with no other covenant but to live!—the goldfinch schooled to pilfer the seeds of the thistle, the flea to explore the dorsal spikes of the drowsy hedgehog! In summer weather can anything be more startling than the growth of the common vegetation, each green bank a garland under the hedgerows, and every retired flower looking, listening, as we human beings, dangerous figures of treachery, pass by?

Yet, say what we may, though we mortals have swept across the earth like a pestilence, over-reaching animal, bird, and fish with merciless intention; though without shame we daily devour the flesh and blood of our fellows, using their skins for gaberdines, their hides for our sandals, and even preserving for our own turn the cup-oil of their joints; yet though we are as ferocious as tigers, as malicious and unstable as monkeys, we still have in us a suggestion of nobility, as though in our begetting we were in truth fortunate to receive a sprinkling of God's very seed. For without prejudice the shadow of a magnanimity rests over the head of the humblest. When you watch an ox and a farm labourer in close juxtaposition, a difference can be detected; a gesture, a look, a tone from the man bespeaking a prouder origin and a wider future.

The alien intelligence of my fancy would be aware of the astronomical constitution of time, with its past, present, and future as one. In every city, in every hundred, in every village, he would see the procession of the generations; in deserts and on grazing grounds; by seashore and by forest glade, he would mark the ephemeral populations springing up like young corn, only a few years later to be rotting out of sight. He would see these violent and obstinate breeds, ignorant, prejudiced, self-obsessed, fretting away their moments, drinking, fornicating, grasping at possessions, and begetting children in wide marriage beds. He would see them hanging themselves, drowning themselves, cutting their throats. He would see them spending their years in obedient acquiescence, sowing seeds, weaving linen, harvesting, contriving tricks for rapidly travelling upon wheels, or manipulating the wave-lengths of the planet's atmosphere for the transference of sound, swift as light. He would see them in gala houses, content to watch pantomimes of their lives, with artificial lights slanting down upon hand-constructed stages, with acted commentaries upon their own existence scrupulously presented, puny, pitiful, passing. He would see them standing at the corners of streets, taking all for granted at the point of weariness, or seated at luxurious tables, picking out olives with finger-nails pink and polished, or peeling off the outer foliage of artichoke flowers, their eyes covertly aware of each other's naked bodies artfully concealed.

Again he would see them very grave, inordinately grave, thronging into assemblies, arguing, demonstrating, full of confidence: self-righteous reformers, pompous and important, they themselves and their causes signifying nothing in fifty years. He would see them crowding into houses of prayer, partaking of barbarous rites with superstitious unction; and a fortnight later at the grave's side with tears streaming down from heads that will be bare skulls in no time at all. He would see them as lovers sharing with the hog, the stoat, and the midge the tremulous and mysterious thrill of creation, boys and girls wandering by the edges of rye-fields, wandering in copses sun-sheltered by hazel-nut foliage tender and thin, the green light through the horizontal leaf plates telling of the fairylands of their dreams. As men and women went to and fro, loving and hating, labouring and cheating, he would listen to their talk and hear them numbering the stars in the heavens, hear them cataloguing their philosophic speculations, hear them meditating upon certain legends and rumours of earth-interested gods.

This alien intelligence could not fail to take note of the strange dispensation of sleep spread wide and far over city and field. For to beasts and birds and the vexed sons of women are vouchsafed recurring intervals of peace, periods of partial oblivion, so as better to resist the pressure of strong life. We may be said to be always dead, wrapped in the lap of eternity, for even during our moment of semi-consciousness, when we look up at the sun with dim blinks for perhaps seventy years, we must constantly have recourse to petty draughts of annihilation.

Slowly the heavy earth revolves, and on the light life-layer of its crust it carries its pitiable burden of individual craniums, drooped and dreaming. The enormous cart-horse, with its nomadic nostril voice, sleeps under the elm tree in the hedge corner where the yarrow grows rank, the swallow also under the tiles. Then once more it is day, and the old man lifts his poll from the pillow, and consciousness draws slowly in upon the being of the old woman; and middle-aged frivolity resumes its season of foolishness; and everywhere, eager and privileged, boys and girls in the prime and flower of their youth open entranced and trusting eyes to the light of the sun.

THE GENIUS OF PETER BREUGHEL

THERE have appeared from time to time in all countries certain artists who have discounted that whole field of religious and metaphysical experience which to many sensitive natures would alone seem to render the rudeness of life tolerable. In England Thomas Bewick might be taken as an almost perfect example of this particular kind of stubbornness; for certain it is that the famous woodcuts of the old north-country coffin-plate engraver would never lead one to suspect that our life, with its libbards, ounces, and gannets, is but an elusive mirage floating uncertainly upon an eternal ocean of abstract thought.

But the greatest of all such mule-headed sons of the sod and the sun is the Flemish painter, Peter Breughel. A single glimpse of any one of his canvases is sufficient to initiate us into the mood and temper of his direct and simple vision. Who could miss, for example, the divine earthiness of his picture of the corn-field now in the Metropolitan Museum of New York City? It has been said that this painting was intended to represent the month of August, and well it may have been, with ears of yellow grain standing solid like *living bread*, and with the labourers reclining "like Gods together" under the trees, symbols themselves, it would almost seem from the bawdy exposure of their codpiece bags, of a crude fecundity under that sublime blaze of noon. And who if not Breughel should be able to portray for us the broad dog-thirsty sunshine of a midsummer harvest-field, born and brought up as he had been on the flat farmlands of Flanders?

If ever a great genius could be said "to have risen out of the soil," it was he, and not, be it noted, from any light soil, but out of the heavy, sluggish, muddy tilth of a low-lying water-logged landscape such as is familiar to us in certain parts of Suffolk. And perhaps the thickness and massiveness of the mud out of which he sprang gives to his genius its particular obstinate quality, that obstinate quality which some of us have come to value very highly, suggesting as it does in these unsettled days so solid a footing. You could as soon hope to drag an overloaded farm wagon out of the slough of two December ruts as alter the destined course of this "original Breughel." Indeed, he follows his essential marrow-deep humour with the lumbering inevitableness of the sails of one of his own windmills going round and round and round. He visited Italy, but alone of all the artists of his time he remained completely uninfluenced by the work of the great masters. He could not be changed. What he liked as a boy he continued to like as an old man. There was about him something of the stout unbending character of a hedge-stick that has been warmed into shape through many winters at a kitchen fire and which, with its root as a handle, retains for ever afterwards its particular look of idiosyncratic intimate *unmanufactured* homeliness.

And yet so terrific was the vitality of the old Fleming that under his hand the very water-soaked clods grow light, the cloven ploughlands illumined, the toilers gay. The frolic-some horseplay of a young colt let out of a stable on a spring morning is in all his country scenes. An echo of jocundity comes from his pictures as insistently as the beating of such an animal's hairy hoofs, undisciplined, unshod, upon soft sap-filled spring mould. Like the unbroken colt his pictures also curvet and kick and tremble and gallop with life. A fish taut with vitality leaps suddenly out of a swiftly moving river, its silver back curved like a new moon. There is not an incident in any picture of Breughel that has not this same "flick" in it.

To stand before *The Dance* or *The Marriage* in the Museum in Vienna is to receive an immediate revelation as to the infinite joy that is our natural heritage. In a flash we acknowledge the wisdom of Villon, of Rabelais, of Shakespeare, of Sterne. If we could live our lives again, with what eagerness and zest would we not eat great yellow custards, go to bed with our brides, and caper light of heel down the village street! In the picture of *The Dance* there is nowhere any suspicion of gravity. Gaily, gleefully, the heavy-footed peasant in the foreground hurries to the scene of merriment, his white teeth bared in an ecstasy of excitement. Close behind follows a middle-aged woman with the lift of a maiden in her legs, for in such company years count for nothing. The bagpipes sound, the frothy beer flows into globose bellies, and great blown-out lips protrude to kiss. All is frolic, all is delight, and each heavy boot with its repeated beating of the ground wears away three months' shoe-leather. It is the same with the marriage scene. How admirable those flat custards look borne into the room on the back of a hinged door! How one longs to partake of one of these same great custards, devil's pancakes, or the most primitive of all sacraments which might—who knows— miraculously initiate us into the divine secret of being happy at such a rate as this. The expression of each face is so original, so full of intimate character that one never forgets it. They become lodged in one's mind with the indelible vividness of the physiognomies of village characters that one knew in one's childhood. How could it be possible, for example, not to remember for ever the look on the bride's face, that look of plump contentment, that look which expresses a simple mind's naïve satisfaction at being permitted to play any part at all in the drama of life, combined with the inarticulate aplomb of the peasant woman who knows without further doubt she has brought her virginity safe into the harbour of matrimony. There she sits with hands folded, a well-fed, unaffrighted, prospective bed-fellow. In their attitudes, as well as in their expressions, Breughel seems to catch each figure as it actually was at the selected moment of time—the pipers with their postures drooping a little from having had to stand up for so long, the child with a peacock's feather in her bonnet sitting with rounded back as with her finger she tastes the favourite dish: the whole room-full of people gutting, guzzling, gourmandising so that their heavy bodies may grow strong to toil, to dance, to embrace under the sun. And they must, indeed, require a superabundance of energy to encounter as merrily as they do the rigours of the wintry landscapes that Breughel depicts for us. How he loves to bring it all before our eyes—the trodden snow, the children's slides, the very poles laid down to corduroy slippery places! The tiniest figure far away under the pollarded willows is complete with life as it tumbles on to its nose, with arms outstretched, no bigger than a snow-fly. A dog is there done to life, humping its back as it befouls the white ground, each separate icicle even, given its own character as it hangs half melting in the sun from the curious tilted eaves.

It is, of course, this detailed realism which to some of us makes his work so attractive, the look of actuality, for example, provoked by a beer barrel which has rolled down a bank and is now frozen into a pond; in short, every accidental process that overtakes the animate and inanimate world, so precious to the sight of those who are in love with life, exactly, punctiliously portrayed.

The deeply personal character of Peter Breughel's paintings is especially seen in his treatment of religious subjects. Even here nothing will budge the old man from his own egocentric preferences, from his uncouth countryman's conception of those rumoured happenings far away in Palestine. The *Road to Calvary* may have been painted in a particular manner for time out of mind, but this fact in no way deters "Breughel of the peasants" from representing it after his own fashion. And so extraordinary was this fashion, and so contrary to any orthodox notion of what took place on that momentous occasion, that the picture when finished gets the painter into considerable trouble. He is brought up before the Inquisition. What right, they ask indignantly, has anyone to envisage sacred history thus? For to Peter Breughel the idea of killing a God must needs suggest on a grand scale the kind of gathering that he had seen come together often enough for bear-baiting. There we see them trooping over the green fields, under the shadow of a Flemish windmill, the sporting raggle-tattle rout of Jerusalem. To-day in England similar crowds may be observed at race meetings. During the eighteenth century doubtless much the same people were to be met with in the lanes and alleys leading to the cock-pits. The more one looks at this careless, amazing, Pack-Monday-Fair procession coming out of Jerusalem "for a bit of fun," the more one wonders at the daring of this artist who in season and out of season insists upon life and yet more life. On a distant hill we see a ring of people watching a place being prepared for the crucifixion, just as I have seen the villagers in Montacute Borough jostle each other to observe the erection of a Merry-go-round. In the foreground near the white skull of a horse we see the Virgin Mary and "the others who followed," huddled together in hopeless, impotent dismay, like a group of tender-hearted cottage women who know that a band of publicans, farmers, dairymen, have dug out a grey badger and are carrying it off in triumph to worry it to death. King Clovis, when he was first told of the death of Christ, the brutal manner of it, remained for some time silent, and then uttered the simple words, "Would I had been there with my Franks!" The shock we get from this canvas is much the same as the shock we get from the record of so naïve a reaction in the face of a matter of such moment, only in the case of the picture the emotion is transposed in that we have scandalously, nay exuberantly, conveyed to us the indecent curiosity, the excitement felt by human beings when they are about to see what some live creature will do in desperate extremity, how a black cat will act as it roasts alive, or what words of terrible implication will issue from the throat of a tortured God hung high on cruciform boards. In the very centre of the picture we see Jesus, already fallen under the weight of the cross, surrounded by a drunken rabble, one of whom has put a foot on the holy rood for the deliberate purpose *of making it heavier*. A few yards further on a rough farm cart carries the two thieves forward, over a stream in the direction of the noisy ring where "all the fun of the Fair" will presently take place.

But it is not until one has visited the Lichtenstein Galleries that one is in a position to estimate in all the profound directness of its comprehension this Fleming's vision of life. It is here that this Sancho Panza of painters gives his final summing up. Here without book learning this Breughel makes a rapid reckoning and sees that the one fundamental fact to be understood about life is death. The greatest of all his pictures tells its story plainly and inelegantly. It affects one's mind as though it had suddenly been vouchsafed to one to inspect the interiors of all the graves that have been since the world began, as though in order to extinguish any last faint hope we might have of a personal immortality we had been called upon to place our hands upon a myriad hollow thigh-bones, and to thrust our fingers into the eye-sockets of a myriad hollow skulls.

To the generations of men peopling for so short a season, like green gullible grasshoppers, the fields of the earth, Death alone constitutes the ultimate truth. With the uncouth realism of a simple mind Breughel pictures the living as being attacked by skeletons. Hung high up on a shattered shell-shocked tree two bells toll out warning of the macabre disaster. The flesh-bereft figures that pull at the ropes below are but two insignificant members of a vast army of invaders who are overwhelming the quick on every side. The miser is taken from his gold, the gourmet from his linen-laid table, the lover from the sweet lap of his lady. Some of Death's soldiers carry a net and go about netting the living as poachers net partridges on a winter's night. Others have set up stockades on each side of an enormous wooden trap such as might be used for trapping sparrows by a stick-house in a back-yard. And to see how they harry and hustle and man-handle their timid ineffectual enemies into the gaping aperture! Supercilious arrogance, the arrogance of Masai invading a camp of Wakikuyu, is the expression most apparent on the living visages of each death's head as they watch the resistance, foredestined to fail, of the "punie habitants."

And already the tumbril of Death is advancing up the street. The head sacristan sits sideways on his black-blinkered grey mare, holding a lantern in his right hand and with his feet resting on the shaft. Well he knows, as indeed his nonchalant listless attitude attests—the attitude of a farm labourer returning to a familiar parcel of ground for the twentieth time with a load of dung—that his employers always win.

The date of Peter Breughel's own death is disputed. He resembled an ancient wych-elm whose very roots sprout saplings. Both his sons became celebrated painters. "Breughel of the Velvet" was a friend of Rubens, and for some time collaborated with him. His granddaughter Anne became the wife of Teniers. Truly it may be said that he was of the stock who repeople the earth with free and magnanimous spirits.

NATURAL WORSHIP

MANY people nowadays find it difficult to pray, above all to invoke supernatural intervention in affairs associated with their own personal advantage. To try to divert even in a small degree the determined sequence of earthly events is an undertaking too easily distressed by doubt. How can it be possible for our pathetic whispers to influence the advance of the great engines of Fate? It is certain that our outcries under impending calamity, however charged they may be with spiritual magnetism, can avail little enough before the undeviating movement of what is to be.

Yet there exists a level of consciousness below the plane of our ordinary life-experience connected with no desire to ward off evil, connected with no desire to conjure good fortune, wherein prayer still remains a legitimate exercise. This spiritual state has to do with the emotion of gratitude. In the spring especially do we feel this animal exultation prompting us at all hours to flex our knees. This is the religion below all religions, the religion that has to do with man's natural awe before the glory of life.

It is from this natural awe that we come to learn that in every breath a man breathes from the chrisom to the shroud there is a sacramental quality. And always it is through the senses, our rabble senses of delight, that this religious mood is quickened. The senses first created thought flashing their undisciplined responses to the flame-like brain.

Those of us who value such poetic awareness more highly than any human experience have learned with thankfulness that these moods are subject to persuasion. They cannot be compelled, but they can be courted. The most simple sight can do it. In the early morning when the dew is still upon the grass the enchantment perhaps will more easily be present with us. At such a time if we go out alone and stand contemplating a common garden flower, a daffodil, let us say, it will not be long before the transport will be ours, stirring our imaginations to a lively apprehension of the solitary existence of so golden an aggregate of atoms, which, virgin of any rude motive, surrenders the breath of its unaggressive being to the hands of the silver dawn. All through the night the plant has grown there in its dedicated plot, its close-set bulb lapped in the cool soil. Men have been lying dreaming in half-darkened rooms, beautiful women have slept with head resting upon open hand, and these ancient flowers of the March winds have been all the time gently responding to the night air, gently swaying in the night, companions to docile, exploring shrew-mice, to bland, silent snails. With the first rays of the sun on the plant's leaves its ethereal spirit is strong enough to summon our convention-blinded souls to this primitive worship. For a few swift moments the sublimity of this yellow weed is apparent and the miracle of its presence, of its creation, shocks us out of our accustomed apathy. When we are before it, our personal cares shed, our personal preoccupations shed, content to envisage its life divorced entirely from our own individual interests, no fald-stool could prompt us better to our devotions. The interplay of its fresh leaves hides ineffable thoughts, and to observe a shadow from one of its green spears lie lightly across a single golden trumpet is to glimpse clearly for a moment an earth dimension of positive fairy-like rapture.

Equally with our eyes our ears can minister to us. There is

nothing more religious than to wait listening at this hour. It is as though the earth were once more new created, as though we were privileged to be cognisant of its stir and quiver outside of our tedious time, as though we were truly "among the green Ilyrian hills" observant of the murmur of the planet during present, past, and future.

Far off comes the voice of a dutiful sheepdog, with the record of a millennial-old domestication in its obedient tone. From a leafless sloe tree the explicit flute of the blackbird's yellow bill dislodges a petal, dainty and white, with a sudden burst of liquid music: and everywhere sound is in the high heavens, shimmering like sun motes at noon as the timeless larks insistently testify to happiness, to happiness, to happiness! It is small wonder when our children show an unwonted exuberance that we accuse them of skylarking, accuse them of trying to emulate these dancing sprites of the air whose singing alone disproves all desperate conclusions. Meanwhile, elbow high about us there is the humming of a diligent employment, suggestive of an extraneous, of a perfected, sun-warmed polity, the polity of the insect world that without protest or apology prosecutes a punctilious husbandry throughout the long summer days.

It is the same at night when under the solemn stars the mooing of cows comes to us from distant fields. In a moment the strange story of man's domination is revealed as we hear these great beasts uttering their lamentations to the immortal night, their huge heads lifted in dolorous unrest as some arbitrary interference with their instinctive natures—a calf taken away or a bull denied them—presses in upon their dim, bovine cognitions. In these voluminous echoes from damp herbivorous mouths there is a heavy melancholy that troubles the circumambient darkness of our planet above the low hedges, above the elm trees that everywhere pierce the obscurity like spires of rogation.

Yesterday in the outskirts of Lulworth Park in a woodland glade, I came upon a derelict carriage. In the years of its neglect it had been brought here as a vehicle for conveying faggots and brushwood to the home-sheds and had been abandoned in this undisturbed place through summers and winters, unused and forgotten! In compact lodgments December snows had settled for weeks upon its faded cushions of Lincoln green, and now on this Good Friday afternoon the first bluebells were visible between the spokes of its wheels deep-set and unrevolving in springy leaf-mould. A gorse bush in bloom grew near and I knelt to smell once more its heavy All-Fools-Day fragrance. My nostrils received a draught of purest earth-life, sweet as pineapple, warm as a linnet's nest, fresh as moorland moss. In a moment my congenital stupidity was gone and I was given a vision of the secret significance of that moment, with the vegetable sap everywhere flowing upward, through the weak stems of the primroses, through each intricate anemone leaf, and along the huge timber boughs of the forest oaks above the brougham, which, like a stately boat stranded in an alien environment, would never again carry dames of fashion, honourable Catholic dames, along the high roads of Dorset.

Taste also will serve our turn, the immemorial taste of baker's bread, for instance, fresh from a hollow oven; the unmistakable, unexpected taste of raspberries; the subtle taste of honey, that most poetical of all quintessences, stored through the winter in architectural cells by bright-eyed troops of devoted filmy-winged liegemen.

As it is with the sense of sight, with the sense of hearing, with the sense of taste, with the sense of smell, so it is with the sense of touch. There is no surer gate into God's chantries here upon earth.

In the highest moment of love, thought itself dissolves away like hoar-frost in the sun. The mind becomes as nothing, the body as nothing, the whole of our being caught up, translated, until it is at one with the incomprehensible mystery that lies behind matter, at one with that incalculable dynamic that is nowhere and yet is everywhere, and through whose agency the star clouds stream across the firmament, the daffodil lifts its head, the swallow chitters, and the ground-ivy delivers up its soul to the ditches. For let them say what they will, it is in the agony and ecstasy of corporeal love, it is under the ascendancy of this first-born of all the senses that mortals draw most near to the quivering secret of life.

A BUTTERFLY SECRET

In a world where all is shifting it is a satisfaction to come upon a countryside that remains as it was. On the Dorset downs, on that noble sweep of coast-land that lies between the Old-Harry-Rock near Studland, and Jordan Hill on this side of Weymouth, it is possible to walk for twenty, for thirty miles across a landscape that is as it has been from the beginning.

Here on these folded hills, whose rounded contours have the strength and simplicity of Old Testament prose, it is easy for one's thoughts to turn, like those of the man of Uz, to ancient questionings. As the long days of sunshine pass by, hour by hour, and the wide cool shadows on the eastern slopes of the downs lie like stable cloths cast over the rounded flanks of enormous sleeping mules, such a mood grows. Of what avail, one asks, has been the passing of the centuries since that old time when the flint-men, whose bones lie under their barrows like the skeletons of curled-up foxes, surrounded their high hills with earth rings? To what end did St. Aldhelm cause a chapel to be built on his wild headland when it has been known and will be known again that the tremulous life of man passes without signification before the throne of the Most High?

And, indeed, as one walks over these downs at night-time, under the fathomless pricked dome of infinity, one receives but one answer. The matter is as plain as a child's sum in a dame's school. Life is its own justification. There is no other aim to it, no other meaning, no other purpose, and if we think otherwise, we are foolish. Let the truth be spoken. Each one of us, each intellectual soul among us, advances steadily and surely towards the grave. Abdel Krim and his Rifis, General Feng and his soldiers, are all marching down that same road—a road that leads to oblivion and that for a thousand years has been trodden by a procession of all nations. Every religion is as brittle as an empty snail shell in dry weather, as quick to disappear as cuckoo-spit in a summer hedge that conceals at its centre no green fly. The secret to be remembered is that nothing matters, nothing but the momentary consciousness of each individual as he opens his eyes upon a spectacle that knows nought of ethics. Let us, as best we may, reconcile our minds to the fact that all our self-imposed tasks, our political engineering, our brave talk have actually, under the shadow of Eternity, no consequence. Our idealism is treacherous. It is a moonshine path over a deep sea. We are cursed souls each one of us and resemble nothing so much as jackdaws flying about the radiant cliffs of God pretending to be sea-gulls.

And yet there is no cause to despair. Merely to have come to consciousness at all constitutes an inestimable privilege. The past is nothing, the future is nothing, the *eternal now* alone is of moment. This is understood well enough by every living creature but man.

Of all the books of the Bible, perhaps the Book of Job expresses best this mood. In verse after verse in this book, the Deity, like some magnificent Leonardo, is made to celebrate in mighty words His own creative achievements. But, as it is with all really great artists, it is evident that He feels a distaste for the static. It is His will to raise up and to cast down, to model and to break into dust.

In America, where human weaknesses are often to be observed in their crudest form, I remember once reading the words "ETERNAL HOME" traced with pretty white-washed stones on a lawn in front of a cemetery gate. They expressed, of course, the unanimous belief of the townsmen of the place in the future life of the soul. And yet as I walk about over these downs, downs that are so far removed from the downs of California, it is continually being brought home to me that these dead men and women by the shore of the Pacific have no longer any form of existence, have been utterly annihilated.

There is only one way to take life, and this we may learn from any common-white butterfly flitting from flower-head to flower-head, from strawberry plant to strawberry plant, content with the sunshine of a summer's day. Yesterday as I rested on the side of a tumulus I witnessed the love-making of two lesser-blues, who were lodged on a long grass which itself was supported by the stalk of a knapweed. Their heads were turned in opposite directions, the one looking towards the sea, the other towards a great inland valley. Their curled trunks below their soft spotted ornamented wings were united, and one could not but marvel at the rare creative genius that could have devised so delicate an expression for these lovely insects to enjoy, on the end of a tasselled grass.

What an eye the male had when I caught sight of it behind a grass seed, a narrow, black, slanting eye, lit up with a kind of arrogant exultation, like the look in the eye of the stallion that drew the chariot of the Great Cham! Gazing into the bewitched eye of this insect, of this most sensitive disciple of Heraclitus, I became instructed that nothing is of consequence but the fugitive fulfilment of each separate existence which has had the good fortune to be called, even for a few moments, into the light of the sun.

THE BLIND COW

BETWEEN Weymouth and Lulworth there is a secluded beach protected on the right by the promontory of Bats Head and on the left by the natural arch of oolite rock called Barn Door or Durdle Door.

Of all the cliffs in the neighbourhood Bats Head is the most favoured by seafowl as a nesting-place. On precipitous ledges formed by tussocks of cliff grass the herring gulls in the spring cluster in great numbers, and if you peer over the dizzy edge of the downs at the egg hatching time, you can see their innumerable young, suggesting small brown owls transported from dusty barns and towers to confront a limitless sky outstretched above the Channel waves glittering bright in the sun.

Higher than these precarious nesting-places of the gulls are certain narrow clefts which the guillemots, for time out of mind, have selected for their stately Mandarin courtships; while dotted about on the bare face of the enormous precipice cormorants may be seen, black satanic images set each one in its appointed niche on this cyclopean temple wall of purest Parian. The rugged crevices of the Durdle Door are less suitable as nesting retreats, and unless the ravens happen to select one of these hollows for their February breeding, the celebrated arch seldom shelters permanent tenants at the time of the spring clamour. Between Bats Head and the Durdle Door, some hundred yards out to sea, there protrudes an ugly rock known to the fishermen below and to the shepherds above as the Blind Cow.

In the summer it is possible for adventurous bathers to swim out to it, but during the winter months the rock remains unvisited, a sullen obstacle to the incoming waves that, week after week, continue to launch their strength upon it, dissipating their power in white fountains of foam that seem to remain for a moment suspended in the air before falling once more into the turbulent eddying waters on the rock's leeward side.

I have seen the Blind Cow Rock at all hours of the day and in all seasons, until it has come to symbolise in my mind the obdurate reality of matter, of determined unimplicated matter, against which the sensitive spray of life throughout the millenniums has dashed itself in vain. The faithful ewe turning her head to smell at the wagging tail of her lamb as it thrusts ruthlessly, repeatedly, for her sweet milk, is under the subjection of the Blind Cow. The lark is at the mercy of the same discipline, as it pours out its thrilling melody for the ears of its mate, couchant below in the grass, her light thighs daintily flexed and the dew of the morning still sparkling upon her dorsal feathers. Nor is the hungry mackerel free, as with a shimmer of its rainbow body it goes sharking after its prey through the curling sea troughs. Yet out of the obedience of the dutiful ewe, out of the poetry in the fragile, crested head of the lark, out of the expert precision of the fish's flashing body it is conceivable that there does rise a certain whisper of hope challenging to the sottish absolute domination of the Blind Cow.

I have often entertained this fancy, especially towards the evening, when, as the sun draws down over the island of Portland, the whole coast-line is held under a vesper benediction, as if the peace of God that passes all understanding was in very truth present and offering some ineffable assurance to the samphire patches, to the sea-kale, and indeed to all the spindrift litter of the foreshore, with its shells and congregated paradise pebbles.

I felt this mood very strongly yesterday afternoon. Never had I seen the Bats Head beach looking more clear, more fresh, its stern Homeric beauty tempered by the grace of a February twilight quick with intimations of the approach of another summer. Soon I knew the flowering blackthorns, the flowering May trees, the flowering elder trees would be offering their provocative opulence in successive progression, until once again the corn-fields would be standing thick with the grain of man's bread, a rustling fairy-forest environment to the mice, to the frogs, to the grasshoppers, and to all those unnoticed insects born to explore with indefatigable accuracy each bended corn leaf.

Surely, surely, cried my mutinous heart to its master, your lifelong conviction is here and now refuted. In the light of such illative feeling, of such inborn confidence, your proud reason must certainly falter and come to confess the possibility of there being, as the faithful affirm, some elusive secret, some spiritual essence in the universe that owes no homage to the Blind Cow.

As I advanced along the noisy shingle, it did seem just then that there had been vouchsafed a positive sign that good hope lies at the bottom of life. During those heightened moments I might have been walking upon a shoal of infinity, upon a sea-bank of eternity, actual but at the same time transcendental.

In this fond mood I approached the diminutive hidden beach overshadowed by the Durdle Door. I now became aware of the presence of a bird under the great rock. It was a guillemot standing alone on the shingle in the afternoon's sunlight. It made no attempt to fly away, and as I drew near I noticed that its body was shivering. Not wishing to alarm it I stood still. I had guessed what was the matter. Except for a few feathers about its neck, all the white plumage of its breast was matted thick with the brown substance of the foul oil with which modern shipping contaminates the sea. As soon as the bird realised that I intended to do it no harm it resumed its task of trying to get itself clean. Periodically it would open its wings and flap them in a fruitless effort to amend the condition of their feathers, though the filaments of each single one, so Dædalus-created for a privileged buoyancy, were in actual fact ruined for ever.

Before now I have carried these unfortunate birds home and have done what I could to clean them with paraffin oil and petrol, but invariably they have died, perhaps from fright, perhaps from despair. I believe that it is best, as Hudson teaches, to leave these children of Nature in the arms of their strong and terrible mother.

As I walked away I could see the guillemot in its simplicity, in its innocency, trying to preen itself with nervous assiduity as though it still thought a few more well-directed pecks would render it once more free to fly over the waves after its odd mechanical fashion. Down to my very marrow-bones I knew for certain that the Blind Cow rules all. Man, deft in contrivance; man, that self-interested, self-absorbed, semi-conscious, semi-civil animal has by this evil heedlessly added one more morsel of misery to the ocean of earth sorrow *and nothing said*. In this sad world what strong arm, human or divine, can be relied upon to rescue the abused, the oppressed, the betrayed?

Let us not be deceived. All life destroys other life to live. This is the natural and irreversible law of existence. Benevolence, malfeasance, it is all one, no difference whatever. To try to contend against stupidity and cruelty is to engage in a cause that was lost from the beginning of time.

In death alone is the hope of the unhappy, in that utter annihilation that brings a fortunate peace to restless life. Make no doubt, there never has been a particle of truth in those simple and beautiful words of Jesus. They represent the passionate wish of a deluded poet, and that is all. "Are not five sparrows sold for two farthings and not one of them is forgotten before God?"

AN OWL AND A SWALLOW

Across the way from my cottage there stands a large barn. It is roofed with slates and, owing to the violence of the gales last winter, many of these are now missing. This spring, for the first time in my memory, two owls chose the building for habitation. They are screech-owls, and every dusk they are to be seen going in and out of a square aperture where a slate should be. I welcomed the arrival of these birds. If you examine one of their pellets it is astonishing to see how many mice they consume. I have counted four mouse craniums in a single ball. They evidently subsist chiefly upon such game, for it is not often that one comes upon a bird's beak in any of these compressed shapes of indigestible fluff. The value of owls against rodent pests was so highly appreciated in the past that it was a common thing for a mediæval builder to provide an especial settling-place for them on one of the great central beams of a grange, a kind of perch, known as the owl stool. Just as we to-day keep a granary cat, so these husbandmen of the old time kept a granary owl.

I visit the barn almost every day. As soon as I open the door, letting in a flood of sunlight upon the golden straw and upon a heap of wooden fodder cages that are stored here for next year's lambing season, one or other of the owls is certain to fly out between the rafters until it reaches a position as remote as possible from the ledge where I suspect the nest to be. Here it will remain and look down at me in that strange intelligent way that belongs to these birds. It looks down at me as though from another world, from some middle-earth where a mortal is a being to wonder at rather than to fear. Our nights are days to owls. While we sleep under domestic quilts they are wide awake flying by hedgerows or over waste places where the poppies appear black in the moonlight, cognisant of the slightest stir, of the faintest shadow, even stooping for a beetle. And something of the strange inhumanity of unnoticed ditches, of unfrequented outhouse corners, has got into the round physiognomy of an owl, so eldritch, and at the same time so sagacious, like an old woman who is both a witch and a midwife.

When I open the door of the barn until the owl settles with the thud of horn striking wood, there is absolute silence. I see its snow-white ventral feathers, its short, terribly competent legs stretched out behind; but, except for this evidence of my vision, I would not be aware of its presence. The flight of an owl is extraordinary to watch, it is so soft. It moves across the dew-wet hay-fields as wavering and noiseless as drifting thistle-down, as if a portion of a white cumulus cloud had become detached and was being blown near to the earth, now up, now down. Who has ever heard an owl beat against the wind or cause a rustle in the air with its lovely barred feathers, softer than eider? Inaudibly each night they move over the shires of England particular to hear the patter of tiny paws, alert to take advantage of a bird's somnolence; occasionally only do they trouble, with their hollow voices, the imaginations of men. One long night-hour follows another, and always this diligent bird is hunting. Round the dusty stable it passes, where cart-horses for generations have startled corn-bin mice with their unexpected stampings; backwards and forwards it flies, present and not present.

A barn has always been the free man's temple. These

buildings have a homely atmosphere about them. The word barn is derived from the Old English bere, meaning barley, and aern, meaning place. Each April a pair of swallows has come to nest in the stable next to the barn. Never were there more faithful lovers. Most of the day they used to spend flying after each other, skimming over the shining slate roofs with darting arrow-like flights; then they would rest for a little, sitting side by side on a fence, making the whole garden glad with their interminable chitter of love. They must have crossed the Channel a half-dozen times backwards and forwards, leaving the chalk headlands when the mushrooms are abundant and returning to them during the weeks when every wood and lane is full of primroses. Punctually each year they must have flown away from the sunny kopjes of Natal, side by side, through untraversed aerial levels. With sharp, long-sighted eyes they glimpsed the argentine gleam of hidden equatorial waters; they looked down upon the broad backs of elephants moving soberly, like dung beetles, over open spaces of dry grass, until at last, in cold darkness, they sighted the revolving light on Portland Bill, as, under the direction of an unerring instinct, wing-weary, they breasted their way over the Race towards the familiar cliffs of the locality where the barn stands.

A few days ago in the late twilight I witnessed this evil. By some black cast of chance the owl had managed to catch one of the swallows. Perhaps she had been injured, or perhaps merely taken off her guard as she prepared herself for sleep. I heard a sudden succession of sharp, scattered cries, and then I saw the owl flying across the barton yard with a swallow in its talons. With distracted shrieks the small companion bird followed, now swooping over the owl, now diving right in front of it in its desperate attempts to rescue its mate. So fierce was its onslaught that I saw the owl swerve unsteadily and, for a fraction of a second, I thought it was going to let go its prey. It was soon upon the roof, however, and a moment later I saw it disappear through the square hole on the sloping surface, as silently, as peacefully as a ghost.

MERTON WOOD'S LUNCHEON

WHEN the Librarian of Merton College wrote to Mr. Wishart on the eve of the publication of my abridgment of Andrew Clark's *Life and Times of Anthony à Wood*, congratulating him on producing a tercentenary edition, nobody was more surprised than myself. Suffering as I always have from "a slowness in apprehending with quickness things," I had entirely missed the fact that my own very personal presentation of the antiquarian's work was destined to appear so opportunely. After such a manner will Providence upon occasions cast down crumbs to wild birds when there is a scarcity of hedgerow berries.

This letter from the Librarian was followed by an official invitation to me from the Domestic Bursar of Merton to attend a luncheon to be given in honour of Anthony à Wood's tercentenary. I felt flattered by the compliment and, in respect for the memory of the dead writer I so much admired, decided to be present at this University celebration.

On my arrival at the College I sent up my card to the Librarian's rooms, and I was received by a scholarly-looking English gentleman. He began to introduce me to a number of dons who stood gossiping by the fire. In Dorset I had felt a slight disquiet about my proposed excursion. I had confessed this misgiving to my brother. "They will have only two thoughts in their heads," he had answered, "their viands and their wine." I was reminded now of his comfortable prediction.

112

"What kind of a luncheon are they going to give us? It is a day for a good hot stew," said one of the group. It might be supposed that such honest talk would have put me immediately at my ease, as, in truth, I think it was intended to do; and so I believe it would have done had not my confidence, still tender, been suddenly destroyed by having it explained that the invitation of which I had been so proud had in reality been intended, perhaps, for my architect brother. A younger don, aware of my discomfiture, detached himself from his companions and came across the room, saying to reassure me that he was quite certain that I had received my invitation "on my own merits." He was an extremely courteous man and my relations with him, then and later, did much to soften a certain resentment that I came to feel towards this ancient house of learning.

The ante-chamber, to which we all presently adjourned, was filled with other dons, and somebody suggested that I should go straight up to the dining hall. I came through its door and down the steps to the dais, where, finding myself standing a little awkwardly among a group of gowned strangers, I thought it best to look for my place at the table, and this I discovered without difficulty and sat down upon a bench opposite to it. Here I drew myself in upon myself as I have observed hedgehogs to do when they find themselves in an unsympathetic environment. From my isolated position I was able to pass several moments in undisturbed meditation upon the scene before me.

After lunch the Chancellor of the University addressed the company. I had never seen Lord Grey before and was impressed by the presence and personality of this distinguished statesman. As I looked at his proud sensitive head the word "religious" came to my mind. There was an innate simplicity about him which might have belonged to a shepherd, and yet something patrician also. He stood out in that hall as aloof and different as a monolith surrounded by a flock of sheep. He spoke with urbanity, but for the most part what he said had nothing to do with Anthony à Wood. He referred to the fact that he had for a long time paid tithes to the College, he recounted anecdotes about Bishop Creighton; and then confessed that he had never read Andrew Clark's volumes, and knew of Wood only through "a recent article in *The Times Literary Supplement*," from which he had gathered that his writings were not suitable for reading aloud.

And so it was with the subsequent speakers. Slowly it became apparent to me that not one of them really appreciated at its true worth the extraordinary originality of this son of their house who had been treated so abominably by their predecessors. They were willing and glad to have acknowledgment of his services as an antiquarian, but they seemed to wish to dissociate the College from the scandal of his outspoken personality. In Oxford, it appears, they have long, long memories. These dons have learned nothing and have forgotten nothing; and the Subwarden of Merton did not hesitate to remind us, who had come together in order to do honour to Wood's memory, that he was *not a Fellow of the College*, and that, though he was a member of the Common Room, he was *turned out of it*. It was clear to me that they actually were half ashamed of this writer whom chance had so closely connected with their house. A reference was made to some Fellow recently deceased—"I never thought to associate *his* name with the name of Anthony à Wood,"—the implication being that, in this parochial pocket of academic prejudice, the comparison was not in Wood's favour, though Anthony à Wood is an historic figure whose "esurient genie" belongs, not only to

Merton or to Oxford, but to the commonwealth of the world's literature.

Certainly I was attending a very half-hearted and grudging tercentenary festival. Why had these dons not appeared in their "scarlet formalities" instead of in their informal gowns? How Wood himself would have eyed this tepid gathering with all his old rancour! "These people," I thought, "are the same that persecuted him when he was alive." They hated him then as commonplace people always hate anyone who is out of the ordinary and who is more spiritually intense than themselves. The passionate zeal that Wood showed in his chosen way of life was beyond their capacity to understand. From the beginning to the end it was in the face of ridicule, carping criticism, and gross stupidity that he carried through his self-imposed, laborious purposes. In actual fact, there was a strange "innocence" in Wood's nature which has never been properly appreciated, and this sensitive quality provoked from those who knew him nothing but derision, contempt, and animosity.

Quite apart from Wood's fearless honesty of thought, quite apart from his hatred of all hypocrisies, he has won his lasting position in English literature because of his quaint idiosyncratic confederacy with antiquity. It was the high prerogative of this solitary and slighted recorder, working day after day in his attic retreat, to hear the wings of the centuries pass over England more clearly than did anybody of his own time and perhaps of any time. The fact that he was such an obstinate and eccentric character made him an object as desirable to bait as a blind bear.

To this day the mention of his name in Oxford provokes either frivolity or moral disapprobation. The truth is, these men of the world have never understood nor cared for his genius. The dons of Merton are still the same, the same, the same! Like one of God's spies, I observed them, watched them, these breathing phantoms sitting solid at their repast, at their refectory tables; some of them deep set in the illusion of the passing moment; others with pallid idealistic faces looking up to heaven; all of them utterly removed from any imaginative realisation of life. One thing only can be relied upon to awaken them,—the shadow of a menace to the security of their ancient foundation; then it is a wonder to see how these "furred cats" and "clerg-hawks" can scratch and clutch. It is not surprising that these Merton dons murmur out their self-interested motto, *Stet Fortuna Domus*, with an almost mystical fervour. Make no doubt of it, they have a brave time in their pleasant garths—a fine view over the flowering meadows, the most perfect miniature library in the world, victuals in plenty at each ting-tang-ting of the dinner bell; wine in the buttery, pipe upon pipe, bin upon bin, tun upon tun!

If the ghost of Anthony à Wood was present in that dining hall hidden away somewhere in the rafters, like a tetchy winter bat too inquisitive to sleep—an assumption far less incredible than are many of the foibles these men teach to the youth of our land—how he, "whose rhetoric served him to curse his bad fortune," would have trounced them after his old unregenerate manner. *His* tercentenary fish dinner, *his* own tercentenary, the tercentenary celebration he had been waiting for for so many, many afternoons down there in the key-cold clay; and it had turned out to be a matter of nothing,—cautious, dull, heavy, stupid; but good enough for "old man A.W. . . . Joan of Hedington will not have him because full of issues; I use to carry lobsters and crabbs there . . .all that is good in my book is not of my putting in . . . I understood not Greek."

When I could escape I went across the quadrangle to

Anthony à Wood's burying-place, and there alone in the chapel knelt upon the cracked slab that marks his grave. Turning my ears from the voices of these latter day "banterers" as they dispersed in the street outside, behind the closed door of this hollow church I tried to call up the old man's spirit, tried to call it up out of the deep grave, to tell it that I, a simple man from the country, with chalk on my shoe-leather; living in a cottage with a rent not worth so much as a thousand groats; an Epicurean from the open fields, too ignorant and too illiterate to grace a book with an index; a guest who had been invited by mistake to the feast, resented with all my being the attitude of these supercilious scholars, as easily fluttered by a few broad expressions as pullets by a handful of chaff, men who still, after the passing of three centuries, could not find it in their hearts to give to the name of Anthony à Wood the unqualified honour that is its due.

AN ANCIENT FRENCH HOUSE

I

A TRAVELLER in France who is on the look-out for what is
secluded and indigenous could do nothing better than to
journey eastward from Lyons until he reaches the small
town of Belley. It is true that the ancient cathedral church
was demolished in the nineteenth century to be replaced by
the white modern building that at present is a conspicuous
feature of the upland valley. But the sleepy market town
retains still an atmosphere of the past. Many of the houses in
its main streets were built in the fourteenth and fifteenth
centuries. I have been admitted through a modest doorway
to enter an interior with beautiful passages, white and
arched like those of a wine-cellar—passages that give
glimpses through narrow, ancient doorways of hidden
gardens, heavy with the damp foliage of sun-sheltered
flowers and trees. Also, if one walks outside the town, it is
possible to imagine that the old city walls are still standing,
so compact, so closely built together, are the houses that
border the open meadows. The reiterated calling of the
peasants, as they encourage and direct their yoked oxen, can
be heard by the shop people in the main streets, by the
children playing at leapfrog in the rue de Baron and in the
rue St.-Martin. Indeed, a wayfarer who explores the country
in the vicinity of Belley will gradually realise that he has at
last reached the France of his imagination, the France that
was before the Great War, before Napoleon's wars, before

the religious wars. The appearance and the manners of the countryside belong to the Middle Ages. Still up and down the stony lanes oxen drag forward small, lumbering carts of mediæval design. Still the wide valley is dotted with women, with old men, and with children standing sentinel, with an infinite patience, through the slow hours, over their few head of cattle. A fence, any kind of protection, would relieve them of their year-long, their century-long, task, but in this district, known as the Bugey, innovations come slowly. The ancestors of these people spent their time knitting in the sun and turning their errant sandy-coloured cows towards the pasturage allotted them—and for what reason should their descendants do otherwise? They no more desire to bring alterations to this uneconomical manner of living than they would wish to alter the appearance of Mont Blanc, whose snow-fields are visible on clear days sixty miles distant. On the higher slopes of the hills, which so softly intersect the lower lands, the grape clusters burgeon and ripen in straight lines, in preparation for coppered vats, while down by the river men make hay out of the rushes that grow in the rough, undrained levels. And how gently the year turns to autumn in these forgotten acres!

In summer-time, of all rivers the River Furens is the most happy. Slowly through the long September hours it winds its way between its silent reeds, with nothing to disturb the unbroken stillness save the rustle of grasshoppers, the fluttering of butterflies, or that most soothing, most harmonious of all possible sounds, the sudden, unexpected splash of a river fish rising to a fly. The rushes of the Furens are tall, and covered with feathery pennants. They sway gently to and fro with the movement of the breeze, or with the slow, persistent current of the cool, deep water. Their stems are filled with white pith, and they can easily be hollowed out to make pipes suitable for the protruding lips of a god.

It happened that I was fortunate enough to be walking by the banks of this river on a late summer afternoon. A fisherman had showed me his catch, and I had held in my hands two beautiful fish. The rims of their eyes were golden, like the rims of eagles' eyes. Their backs, when I rubbed away a few silver-white scales, revealed themselves as possessing an emerald peacock sheen, smooth and slippery, and smelling of that indescribable smell that belongs alone to fresh-water fish.

How the great Montaigne would have relished the scene, I thought, had he in his journey to Rome passed through this ancient valley. When I think of the French countryside, it is always to his writings that my mind reverts. How he loved to observe its sluggish life unroll before his indolent scrutiny— season merging into season, the grape harvest into the days of mud and rain, the time of sowing into the time of budding. There is no château in France that I would rather see than Montaigne's château, with its tower and chapel, as they say, still standing. How extraordinary to enter the chapel where the good man, his wits awakened with red wine from his buttery, would indulge in his wry devotions! Montaigne, indeed, was in my mind when I left the fisherman to follow under some poplars, which bordered the riverside meadow where men and women were so diligently employed in piling the rough fodder on to their squat carts. I did not know that I had only to pass the last tree and there would appear high up on the hillside, with a command of the valley as far as eye could see, a veritable duplicate of the famous manor dedicated to the Muses. "What is that château over there?" I asked a woman who, islanded in her wooden sabots was watching her cows. "It is the Château de Vieugey, mon-

sieur," she answered. "It is very old—so old that the period
of its building is forgotten." I noticed that her tone seemed
hushed as she referred to the antiquity of the place. To
simple people the past carries weight, is to be revered. They
regard all that comes out of it with religious awe, as they
might regard relics from the obscure recesses of some
venerable sanctuary. "Great seigneurs lived in it once, but
now it is owned by those who till the ground with their
hands."

II

Slowly I mounted the winding road that ascended the hill
beneath the walls of the place. I found a portion of the great
gateway that had been at the entrance of the courtyard still
standing. The door of the farm upon which I now knocked
opened into a round tower built of enormous stones. Above
the mullioned lintel a headstone protruded, chipped and
shattered. Presently I heard the sound of steps, and I was
admitted forthwith. The woman who had opened the door
proved to be the farmer's wife. She was very affable, but
could tell little of the history of the dwelling. "My mother
knows; you must ask her," she said. "It is a sad story." She
took me to the top of the tower, where, through gaps broken
in the masonry, I looked out at the opposite mountains, and
at the peasants working in the fields, with their yoked oxen
lugging burdened wains slowly behind them between the
small round foreign hay-cocks. She took me through great
halls with faggots and out-of-use farm implements lying on
the floors, and with their spacious stone fireplaces littered
with hay and straw. Some of these rooms were fitted with
stone seats in alcoves on each side of iron-barred windows.
What men and what women of the old days, dressed in their

stiff, proud garments, had rested on them? In these rooms, how many children had been brought up and taught to control their insubordinate wills!

In yet another wing of the place was a small square chamber—the chapel. Near the door was the stoup for the holy water, now half full of owl's pellets. Here it was that the owners of the land had expressed each morning and evening their unsuspicious, mediæval faith in the Christian religion.

When we came back to the kitchen we found a man there, the farmer, of enormous stature, come in from the fields, his blue shirt open. I never have seen such a chest—it was hairy as a gorilla's. And there rose from the fellow a rich, rank, animal smell, like that which rises from a cow stall or from a stable. He was very friendly. I asked him how it was I had seen so many ash trees pollarded, and he explained to me that in the dry season they supplement the winter's fodder with their faggots. Both cattle and sheep fatten on dry ash leaves, but the faggots have to be got ready for the cows, whereas the sheep nibble the leaves adroitly and take care not to hurt their mouths with the twigs or splintered branches. To bring home the point to my intelligence, and for want of words, he simulated with his own jaws the clumsy, unseeing manner of eating that belongs to a cow, and the mincing eclecticism that a sheep displays when feeding. "I wish I could speak another language than French," he suddenly said. "It is useful." I was surprised at hearing this uncouth peasant give utterance to such a desire. "Every hedger and ditcher," I thought, "has now learned the value of culture." But it turned out that his words were prompted by a very practical consideration. The man had been called up in the Great War to defend France. He had a mother and father and a wife and four children dependent on him, and it was with the greatest reluctance that he left the old château. At the front he picked up a few words of German from a prisoner who was a farmer and liked to talk with him about country matters. A little afterwards, when his troop had been ordered "over the top," he had suddenly found himself, in the confusion of the battle, confronting one of the enemy in a narrow dugout. Each was about to shoot the other down, when the Frenchman called out in the few words of German he had learned, "Brother, let us not kill. Let us return alive. Let us shake hands"—which they did with tears of friendship. "Ah, monsieur," he said, "it was those few words that saved me, that allowed me to come back and walk in front of my oxen. Who would have been the gainer if we had both been killed! As it is, I am still blessed by feeling the sunlight on my shoulders."

Extraordinary how the simple desire to get home to his family had taught this son of the soil a reasonableness of vision not often to be attained even by wiser heads. I asked him about the château. He knew nothing. He had heard that it once belonged to two brothers who killed each other. His old mother would tell me. She was out with the cows in the field next the river. He would show me where—and he led me to the window and indicated a tiny black speck, small as a jackdaw, far away below. Where we stood was his kitchen sink, and I noticed how its surface was polished like marble, that surface sloping down to a drain of ancient workmanship that led out to a stone gargoyle. "Voilà, voilà ma mère," he kept repeating, and, as I stood by him with the sour-sweet hayseed sweat of his muscular body in my nostrils, I was able to appreciate the depth of his affection for his secluded locality, peopled with the familiar characters that he knew, and where in the long twilight there would come against his face puffs of wind cooled by the dew of numberless vineyards, and by the water contained in the huge stone troughs, large and oblong as abbots' coffins, out of the mossy hollows of which, each morning and evening, his great subject beasts raised their dripping muzzles.

I found the mother sitting on a rush-bottomed chair in the middle of the meadow, near a row of poplars. She was an old woman dressed in black, and was occupied in knitting a sock out of rough, unbleached wool. I asked her for the story of the house. "I will tell you," she said. "It was long ago, and the property in those days was in the possession of a family called Rigaud. The last heirs were two brothers. There had been a fête, an entertainment, at the château, and these young men, after it was over, went to rest out here, near where I sit, under a large mulberry tree that now is cut down. They slept, and the stars came out. Presently an owl awaked them, calling its call in the branches above their heads, and one brother remarked to the other, 'I wish I had fields as large and wide as the firmament,' and the other replied, looking at the night sky, 'I wish I had cattle as many as the stars.' 'What would you do with so many oxen, brother?' 'Drive them to graze in your meadows.' Then the other brother answered fiercely, 'If you sent them to graze in my fields I would cut off their legs.' And the other replied, 'If you served me as mower, I would serve you as butcher.' And a quarrel rose out of the dispute of so violent a nature that they drew their rapiers and ran each other through the body. When the great new church was built, at the time I was a child, they dug up the bones of these two unfortunate ones who were buried in the same grave, and behold! none could tell them apart. That is the tale as my husband used to tell it, but in the library of the college they have papers. It would be best to go there. My husband loved the place. When he was so poor that he had to work for another he would come for miles so that he could dig in the garden under these old

124

walls." At the thought of her good man tears began to trickle down her cheeks, which were brown as nut leaves in autumn. "He was a kind man, my husband was. He would make the coffee in the morning, and at any hour of the day would come into the court and say, 'What can I do, Gabrielle, to help?' He was an innocent, and the good God took him."

III

The next morning I consulted a priest at the College of Lamartine, and after some negotiations had sight of the necessary documents. Little by little I filled in the old woman's story from recorded facts. The château was built about 1303. It was first held by the family Rigaud. They were of importance in the neighbourhood, and one of them, towards the end of the fifteenth century, became the Archbishop of Rouen. This prelate presented the cathedral with a monstrous bell, which, in his honour, was called "La Rigaud"—and so heavy was it that to ring it a man had often to revive himself with drink, which gave birth to the expression, "Drink while pulling the Rigaud." It was the two great-nephews of this archbishop who killed each other in the way related by the old woman. They were twins, and though they loved each other dearly they would often quarrel. They looked so much alike that even their parents could hardly distinguish the one from the other, Gaston de Pompée from Pompée de Gaston. Until the rebuilding of the cathedral church there was to be seen near the high altar a Renaissance monument. It marked the place where the two boys were buried. It was found necessary to remove the tomb, and when it was opened two skeletons were seen with bones intermingled. In this way the truth of its Latin inscription was proved—*Mens una, cinis unus.* Mind one, ashes one.

I revisited the château once more before I left Belley, and my memory of it remains clear as I saw it for the last time—that house with its tragic story, standing in silence above the wide enshadowed valley of the River Furens. It was here that those ill-fated children used to pursue, between the gnarled stocks of the grapes, the great green lizards peculiar to the country. And above the small red tiles of the château are still to be seen, significant of this land of wine, along the ridges of the upland slopes, uneven rows of vineyard stakes.

A HOUSE OF CORRECTION

IT has been shown that if dogs, under experiments that have to do with their conditioned reflexes, are presented with problems beyond their powers of solution, there is set up a neurosis so acute that several weeks are required before the spiritual health of the animal is re-established. It is possible that much of the nervous instability characteristic of human beings can be explained in the same way, seeing that it is our destiny to pass this life under the shadow of certain insoluble metaphysical problems. Maurice Maeterlinck says somewhere that of all living creatures dogs alone are happy, because they are fortunate enough to see plain in the flesh a living god and to have this insistent yearning satisfied.

If this is the case, how careful we should be in no way to betray so touching an illusion. I myself have never been a great lover of these animals. I am afraid of the fierce ones of their species, and discomposed by the others, whose supplicating manners seem to put upon me obligations, such as fetching food and water, or taking them out for exercise. Now and again, however, it has happened that the personality of a particular dog so far invades my sympathy that it seems to separate itself from the lower creation. Recently I have had a good example of this.

I have taken rooms for a year in a cottage on the Sussex Downs, and as the house is very isolated it is necessary for me each week to fetch my own butter. In the back-yard of the dairy farm I visit there lives an old shaggy sheep-dog. He is always chained. His brown eyes that look up through his matted hair possess that particular expression of moral goodness that is so appealing. They suggest a capacity for utter devotion, for utter fidelity which, in a world where all is at hazard, and where feeling is so often frivolous, is very moving. The dog's name is Tinker. His kennel stands directly below the dairy wall. On the inside of this wall all is spotlessly clean. The empty milk pails collected here shine in the afternoon light as though they were silver shields, and the brick paving upon which they rest has obviously been swilled down with water and scrubbed, scoured, and brushed every day. On the other side of the wall, in the yard where the dog lives, it is a very different matter. Here the cattle that are driven in and out of the sheds at milking-time have churned up a fine slush. If it were the ordinary midden litter of a cow barton it would not be so bad, but it is a liquid mud, two or three inches deep, of the splashing kind that is often to be found outside pigsties. Tinker's kennel, with its roof patched with an old piece of tin, has been properly bespattered with this filth, and when he stands on his hind legs against the wall, as he very often does, you can see that the grey hairs that hang from his back and shanks are held together in solid elf-locks such as could only be removed with a good sharp pair of shears of the kind that I was accustomed to use for "dagging" sheep in Africa.

It was this very habit that the dog had of standing upright against the wall that first caused me to take notice of him. I was coming out of the low whitewashed cheese-room with my three rolls of butter wrapped up in white, crisp grease-paper, when I caught sight of two eager paws appearing over the tiled coping. The animal seemed so friendly when I stroked his broad forehead that I went into the yard and round to the kennel. He had evidently been trained not to jump up, but I realised, as he sniffed eagerly at my knees and rubbed his head against me, that his body, under its unkempt hair, was trembling with excitement at having someone come to his kennel and take notice of him. The kennel, a large one, being absolutely plastered with the mud of the yard, presented a very sordid appearance, and there rose from the ground about it a strong odour of dog's urine and dog's dung. I felt sorry for this sheep-dog, and my consciousness of his evil destiny was accentuated by the fact that the chain attached to his collar was an exceptionally heavy one, with iron links of an enormous size, more suitable for chaining a man than a dog. Indeed, it was just such a chain as one sees in pictures of negroes manacled together during the terrible "middle passage" of slave-trading days.

After this, whenever I came for the butter, usually on Tuesday afternoons, I never failed to go round to the kennel, and the dog used to be on the look-out for me, so that the moment he heard the click of the farmyard gate he would be out of his kennel, demonstrating his excitement by putting his paws up to the top of the wall, by wagging his tail, and by uttering ingratiating guttural noises of brute beast affection. Once, before I left my cottage, I remembered to put some food in my pocket, the drumsticks from a chicken I had eaten for my luncheon. He devoured the stringy legs of the fowl in the most ravenous way, crunching them up wholesale in the mud outside his kennel door.

A week ago I went to fetch the butter as usual. That Tuesday happened to be one of those days in January that give unmistakable promise of the first stirrings of the spring. There was something tender, almost ethereal in the air, an indefinable lightness suggesting the first movements of a young girl waking from sleep, as though the eyelids of the earth were delicately lifting in a state of half-realised consciousness.

In the hedge of the green lane leading from the downs I noticed there were lambs'-tails out, their golden tassels suspended against the leafless thorns and elders. Skylarks were rising from the cold fields for those first low flights they practise when it is still winter. The afternoon's sunshine was spread abroad over Sussex with the gentle grace that belongs to this time of the year, when the sun is still gathering to itself its new strength. Soon the days would slide by and the anemones would be out in the spinneys, the marsh marigolds out in the withy beds, and the swallows back in the barn, and the cuckoo's voice would be calling through the raw impassioned air of April dawns. As I anticipated the sensitive progress of the swift seasons still in the future, the largesse, the benison of life seemed infinite. It was impossible not to bless God for our blood and quick breath. On the simplest plane the reward of life seemed incalculable. As I continued to walk over the wintry grass on one side of a deep cart rut, my whole being was stirred with admiration, with adoration for the mystery of existence. So fond, indeed, was my mood that it went out of my head that there was such a thing as evil in the world.

Coming across the last field separating me from the farm, I passed the dairyman spreading out heaps of dung that had been unloaded in symmetrical lines. I stopped to say a few words. He was a powerful, hard-working-looking man. "You are giving this ground a good dressing," I said. "Yes," he said. "If I'm not mistaken you'll see a terrible sight of mowing grass in this here mead come June-time." Immediately his words threw me back again to my recent mood, as in my mind's eye I saw the hayfield of his vision in all its plenary beauty edging up to the very walls of his thatched homestead, with the red flowers of the sorrel swaying above the clustered grass heads, with white butterflies zigzagging wantonly over them, and with swallows searching for flies through the soft air of summer.

I had now reached the yard gate. This time I heard no sound of Tinker's heavy chain moving, so I concluded he was not in his kennel, and made my way over the garnished bricks direct to the cheese-room. "I did not see Tinker," I remarked to the dairyman's wife, as, with her back turned towards me, she was wrapping up my pats of butter, yellow and sweet-smelling as cowslip balls. "He is there," she said, "but he got himself into trouble this morning. He got loose and wandered off to the village. We were forced to send a boy after him, and he was given a taste of the stick."

As soon as ever I could I went round to the kennel. I called the dog. There was no response. Kneeling down, I put my hand into the dark tunnel of his dwelling. I felt the hard bone of his broad forehead, and began to stroke it. An aura of profound dejection seemed to emanate from this dismal house of correction. The dog's spirit had evidently been so broken that he feared even to look at the afternoon's sunlight lest the protruding of his rough head might be interpreted as a wish for freedom. I was convinced that some shocking violence had been done to him. I could not be mistaken. I was looking into a hole of despair. Alone in the squalor of his soiled prison, with his bruised limbs lying on vermin straw, I knew that the very nature of this dog, in all its trust and simplicity, had been brutally outraged down to the depths of its perplexed consciousness.

Two or three times I tried to coax him, tried to persuade him to look out of his kennel door, but he would not. Lying in loneliness, his animal spirit had abandoned its will in abject and absolute submission to the inexplicable wishes of his arbitrary master. Surely, I thought, my mood of the lane and of the field was utterly false and could never return.

131

Then, sudden as the theophany on the road to Damascus, as I knelt with my soul in hell, *it was with me again*, for, although no sound came from the sheep-dog's foul gaol, a rough tongue had begun to lick the back of my hand.

OF EGOISM

NOT long ago I found myself standing in the small hall of the Bull at Cambridge. Twenty years had passed since I had walked to the Senate House to take my degree, twenty years had intervened since my feet, with the light step of youth, had gone in and out of the heavy gateway of what Matthew Arnold once described as "a collegiate-looking building opposite." My companion had left me and I awaited his return in a mood of suppressed excitement.

There it all was before my eyes exactly as it had been, and here was I actually standing in the doorway of the ancient hostel that had been known to my father, to my grandfather, to John Milton, and to God only knew how many men of the old time before them. Presently I could contain myself no longer, and noticing a porter quite near me I addressed him in the following manner: "It is twenty years since I was last here." The porter was an old man who had about him that look of decrepit agility which one often observes in servants who make a living out of lifting, hauling, and rolling about on their brass-tipped corners the heavy travelling trunks of rich men. He had a bald head and a demeanour of gossipy obsequious impertinence. Yet as I ventured my too innocent remark I never for a moment suspected that it was this antiquated "boots" who was destined "to put me wise" in a way I should never forget. No sooner had I spoken than I observed a peculiar expression pass over his features, an expression of deferential ennui, an expression that, before he had uttered a word, made me recognise him philosophically

133

as my master. When he did open his lips it was to tell me that the day before a gentleman had come in who had not been back for twenty-seven years, and the day before that another who had not been back for thirty-five years, and before that someone who had recognised *him*, the porter, who had not been back for forty-nine years. "Gentlemen are always coming back, Sir; we get them all the time, Sir; every week, every day they are coming back, Sir."

He had said enough. I knew at once that I had been caught nursing that childish illusion which tricks us into fancying that the experiences of our own personal life can be of any real interest to our fellow men. It is, of course, a most absurd notion. And yet how many of us will stumble into this man-trap, supposing in our provincialism that it is an easy matter to solicit the attention of strangers to the incidents of our life dramas, when in reality the only chance we have of catching the ear of the porters of this world is by recognising *them first* and little by little to entrammel their egoism, so that, like billy-goats with white collars round their necks, they may feel it no hardship to be conducted down the road of our own romantic wayfaring!

But although I was careful not to give myself away again that afternoon, I did, I confess it, experience the most singular emotions. There was Corpus before my very eyes with the elm trees of "Cats" standing on this side of the street just as I remembered them in the little engraving which used to hang over the chimney-piece, half obscured by paper spills, in the dining-room of Montacute Vicarage—in that little engraving in a black frame so often examined by me during the suspended interval of time between the ringing of the bell for prayers and the sound of the study door opening. And as I looked at the legendary familiar prospect a hundred memories invaded my mind like shadowy birds settling to roost, one after the other, in an ivy tod on an old wall.

Once more as a freshman I stood on Queens' bridge by the side of my father and heard him say, "I have much to be thankful for, to be alive still when so many have died," words which I must have unconsciously treasured for the reason that I now cannot dissociate that portion of the river which flows past the college of Erasmus from them, though at the time, I am convinced they could have seemed of little moment, so eager was I for life, and so inaccessible must I have been to any hint as to the transitory nature of existence.

How happy it were if one could, when one had a mind to do it, put a finger against the long ticking minute-hand of Time! I should like to live it all over again. I would gladly once more suffer the blighting sense of humiliation I felt one autumn afternoon as I came out of the Union in Norfolk jacket, fresh as dry heather, and was accosted by a supercilious youth at the gate who asked me if I would be kind enough to tell him what horse had won the ——, naming a famous race. Never to this day have I forgotten the look of disdain, the look of urbane, commiserating impatience that flickered across his face as he turned away, leaving me to pursue my direction past Trinity, a "Corpus blood"—a blood who was no blood! They were lovely days and it was wonderful to come up from the cow-trodden, rain-soaked woods and meadows of Somerset to the cobbled quadrangles of the University, to exchange the decorous winter tea-table at home with the heavy dining-room curtains fast drawn, and toast and eggs and old-fashioned scones, for wild nights in the Old Court with Christopher Donaldson drinking draughts of neat whisky and daring the devil to snatch us to hell.

By the end of my first term I had met Louis Wilkinson, that gentleman from Suffolk whose emancipated spirit has done so much to free my mind of cant. I went to take tea with him in his rooms at John's on the other side of the river. Ralph Straus was there and I spoke so freely, so extravagantly, so blasphemously that Louis Wilkinson, I remember, got up and "sported his oak" lest some eavesdropper should cause him to be cast out of Cambridge. From that first afternoon we were always together, walking and talking and jesting, intoxicated with life! It was Louis Wilkinson who introduced me to J. C. Squire. I remember the shock-headed knave of hearts. He used to sleep all the day and was only to be met with when the sun was going down; shuffling about the cloisters in slippers and peering out like an owl from a holly bush all bemused with speculations. In those days he used to feed on knowledge as an ant-bear feeds upon ants at midnight. This was long before he became converted. Louis Wilkinson remained always unintimidated by prevailing prejudices. From the moment he was taken from his mother's lap he confronted the world with unabashed aplomb. Like a true philosopher he has always been prepared to discuss anything at any time. And in those days it seemed that we could not bear to be separated, and indeed to this hour my spirits are never more "gay" than in his company.

When I had left the Bull and entered into Corpus as far as the Old Court, renovated now to look like a picturesque Devonshire almshouse with the ivy that my grandfather planted removed and with a pretty tablet set up to the memory of Kit Marlowe, how I was haunted by the figures of the past! It seemed incredible that in the space of twenty years death could have conducted the stooping forms of so many lusty dons out of the college gates. Old Fanshaw! he was never one to foster false upward-bounding skylark ideals. There was an honest man if ever there was one! With his grey hat and well-balanced belly how he would move towards his rooms in the corner of the New Court sublimely unmindful of the daisies shining in the grass at his side! And how kindly the old man was, and how he could laugh, and what sound reins he had for absorbing old port from the cellarage! Many a time have I stood to watch him, speechless with admiration at the spectacle, get up into the old horse-drawn tram, a moving monument of jocund dignity, on his way back to Shelford. Shelford! Who now wanders down those paths where "Fanny" once walked, black skull-cap on head, and to what alien fields has sweet Cousin Amy been driven, fields far removed from the pleasaunce of her childish memories, the security of which, and the May-time beauty of which, even proximity to the railway could never destroy?

And the old master of Corpus, that relic of a great century, grown pathetically feeble—I have often felt proud to think that I entered the College when he still reigned at the Lodge. I used to look at his refined, ecclesiastical, academic face as he tottered into chapel, like a very ancient sheep that was being preserved for superstitious reasons by a set of vigorous priests, and feel upon my brow the breath of ninety forgotten summers, of ninety forgotten winters. Once or twice the old man took a part in the service, his quavering voice, treble as the voice of a centenarian cottage woman, pronouncing the word "humble" without its aspirate, as though in the old times out of which he came the God of the evangelical party had been a God to be feared indeed! With what a different glance I regarded the Rev. ——, a pinched, fanatical would-be saint of the Anglican persuasion, with the narrow, limited vision of a Bishop's chaplain, who once pursued me out of chapel, exasperated past endurance by my ill-behaviour as I shogged off in my spotless white surplice towards my own godless rooms in the Old Court.

But about the Dean there was no nonsense. I can still see the look in his left eye slanting down upon us, as I knelt at the side of Alf Wood scribbling bawdry in my hymn-book, a look entirely devoid of petty spite, but firm, confident, circumspect as the look in the eye of a powerful toad, well versed in the statecraft of its kind, who watches with unclosed lid a tough-skinned devil's coach-horse crawling about under a dock leaf just out of reach of its tongue.

Many were the honoured figures to whom in my uncouth ignorance I failed to do homage. Mr. Charles Moule, there was a true scholar, a scholar with the countenance of an English gentleman and the delicate, self-effacing spirit of a child of God. And the Rev. Charles Archibald Edmund Pollock, the most lovable of them all, he who, under a signed portrait of Robert Browning, used to instruct me in the difficult art of solving algebraical problems and who had, and still has, a heaven-sent congenital incapacity for treating life with the rude rigour it requires. Willingly enough, if it were possible, would I put myself once more under the direction of these men. They belonged to the old Corpus, to Corpus before it grew grand, before it became associated with the High Church party and celebrated Mass at dawn with fashionable applause.

I have often regretted that I made such an ill use of my three years' residence. I spent far too much of my time hanging about tavern doors, and that's the truth! What demon persuaded me to go carolling drunken ditties night after night? With such immemorial turf under my shoes, turf shining bright in the moonlight, and with such historical stones all about me, how came it that I could behave so badly? Seldom, too seldom, during those insubordinate terms did I ever attain to that fortunate mood of consciousness when a mortal soul, winged with the fluttering, poised wings of a kestrel hawk, surveys life with inspired vision. Balked of academic distinction by ignorance and indolence, I must needs resort to the prerogative of a plough-boy and endeavour to indent my identity by means of the letters of my name cut rudely into the fine old oak which surrounded the fireplace of my rooms.

"Now that you have got your degrees what do you intend to do with them?" remarked the present Bishop of Derby as he led two of us towards the Senate House. Like sturdy hedge-rogues whose ears have been cropped, walking by the side of a duck-pond constable, we answered not a word. We had no conjectures to offer as to our future. But the query stuck to my memory for many years after, for I very soon discovered that it was by no means an easy thing in this world to come honestly by a good pair of breeches; though the manner by which we achieve the difficult feat when once it has been achieved, furnishes a subject of unflagging interest to each of us, as I had an opportunity of observing many years later when I watched my friend Doctor Watson, himself a man of substance, listening with deferential docility to a Detroit citizen explaining to him in detail what a "nice little business he had built up." "And how many patients have you on your file, Doc?" I heard him ask before settling down to resume his story, an interpolated interrogation recognised by everybody in the small railway compartment as requiring no answer, merely being interjected by the stranger as a preliminary to a prolongation of his favourite topic. So, I thought, as I stood by a washstand in that swaying Chicago express, even the loquacious storekeeper is conversant with the elementary principle of life which teaches us, in human intercourse, to go angling for each other's egos as though they were little white minnows flashing about in dark, deep, cloudy waters.

OUT OF THE PAST

A RARE occupation it is to vex our minds with trying to recreate a living, visible background for events in our country's history, a rare thing to envisage with undimmed mental eye just exactly how the chalk cliffs of England looked, with thyme and viper's bugloss in flower, when Cæsar visited our island; to recapture in retrospect the very smells of the great Hampshire forest on the morning of William Rufus' death; to hear across fields enclosed for hay the sound of the rebeck as the country villages rejoiced over the return of Charles Stuart.

But quite apart from such imaginative pastimes, which are, indeed, common to all of us; each family, however modest its origin, possesses its own particular tale of the past —a tale which can bewitch us with as great a sense of insistent romance as can ever the traditions of kings. The years lived by our father before he begot us have upon them a wonder that cannot easily be matched. Just as we feel ourselves half participant in the experiences of our children, so in some dim way do we share in those adventures of this mortal who not so long ago moved over the face of the earth like a god to call us up out of the deep.

Often it is the name of some particular place, some historic city with tilted roofs and clustered chimneys, some market town or wintry hamlet, that is associated with this transfigured world before we were born. We grow up with scraps of hearsay about the place for ever in our ears, the very repetition of the accustomed syllables creating presently an assured legend, a legend that takes soon an important part in the substance of our minds.

In the annals of my own family it is the Dorset village of Stalbridge that has held our imagination in fee. Ever since the days when our father would visit the nursery before going down to his tea in the dining-room, the word "Stalbridge" has carried in its utterance a significance outside the commonplace. Stalbridge! The old china tea set came from Stalbridge. It was at Stalbridge that a cup of coffee used to be left in the oven over-night so that it might be warm for my father in the early hours of the morning when, as a boy, he set out to fish for pike in the still black river pools of the Stour. It was in Stalbridge Vale that my father had found all the rarest specimens in his collection of birds' eggs, in the collection which he preserved so carefully all through his long life in the three lower drawers of the cabinet in his study. It was to Stalbridge that he had gone, half across the county, in his great age, when, rendered dumb as an animal by the merciless years, he had suddenly, without warning, left his servants in his house at Weymouth. Hour after hour passed and still he did not return, this aged, inarticulate clergyman, who was so old that he had almost forgotten how a man puts bread into his mouth. It was to Stalbridge that he had gone, to the beloved rectory where he had played with his brother.

What manner of call had he received, imperative and not to be denied, to return unto that place from whence he came? Far away over the seas as I was at the time, I have often wondered whether I could have borne to have found him, this old man, my father, advancing with deliberate intention, with intellectual intention, along the green leafy lanes of Dorset. Should I have had the temerity to divert him from his dedicated pilgrimage with the cry of "Father!" as he went forward, this octogenarian who was lost and yet who knew every stile, every ditch, every shard, along the way he was taking?

It is exactly ninety years since my grandfather, who was born at the end of the eighteenth century—was born, indeed, but five years after the death of Dr. Johnson—came first to Stalbridge to take possession of the fattest of the Corpus livings. And in the circle of those years my father has lived to a great age, and to-day lies buried hip-bone to hip-bone by the side of my mother in Somersetshire clay.

For the first time in my life I visited Stalbridge last Whitsuntide. I set out upon my adventure in bright June sunshine. Hardly had I descended upon the deserted village platform when I felt come over me a strange glamour. Although for sixty years no member of my family had lived in the village, yet as I came up the street each crooked, mute paving-stone seemed to keep back a memory. I entered the churchyard, and there under the tall holly, with rose trees at its foot, was the flat stone marking my grandfather's grave. There he was lying, this other octogenarian, hip-bone to hip-bone with *his* wife. Presently I opened a side gate and entered Stalbridge Park. It was noon. I found myself in a hayfield. As I ate my fruit, under the shadow of a group of West Country elms, ninety years seemed to me to shrink to the proportion of a day.

With the ancient timber standing in the mown grass, with the protecting wall of quarried slabs set up like tombstones about the meadow, familiar to me from many an old faded water-colour in the album at home, the prospect before me was exactly the same, and I knew it, as it must have been when, as a young girl, Queen Victoria sat upon the throne of England. Here through these sweet-smelling pastures my grandfather must have walked on many a summer evening;

here my father must have come as a boy on many an early spring morning in search of the brittle eggs of the far-off ancestors of the birds which crossed and recrossed my vision in the trembling gnat-burdened air between tree and tree. Out of the stones of the old sheep-washing pool, now fallen into decay, grew herb-robert and silver-weed, flowers so familiar, so actual and inevitable to the experience of my own life, that it seemed impossible that these simple tokens of the countryside as I knew them could ever have adorned in the same matter-of-fact way the nooks of this rural structure on those occasions when my uncle and my father had stood to watch the busy activities that used to take place here in the old days.

I left the park and entered Wood Lane, a hesitating narrow lane which runs above the village. I knocked at the door of a thatched cottage. The woman who answered me gave me cool water to drink from her mossy well. She knew nothing of my grandfather, but told me to go to an aged woman named Maria at the end of the street. Old Maria had nearly lived out a century and yet her mind was still clear. She took down a book, a thin book on religion, kept carefully all these years, with my grandfather's writing on it. "You yourself be terribly like to him," she said. "I can mind the old gentleman as though 'twere yesterday; I can most see 'en now come down the street with half-crown in flat of hand. On one of the young gentlemens' birthdays we would go up to the house and dance before 'en. I do carry the ditty in head to this day." And this old woman, whose face had retained through all her years so much refinement, sang to me these simple words:

> "Children go to and fro
> In a merry, pretty row.

Footsteps light, faces bright,
'Tis a happy, happy sight.
Swiftly turning round and round,
Do not look upon the ground.
Follow me, full of glee,
Singing merrily."

And as I gazed upon this frail human being, so purely winnowed by the harsh flails of life, I felt a deep love surge up in me for the old creature who still carried in her head the memory of the dancing days of her childhood under the mulberry tree in the rectory garden of Stalbridge eighty years ago. There she stood before me, backed by her cottage ornaments, her small head swaying a little as she repeated the words of the rhyme. When I turned to go, tears were falling down her cheeks and were in my own eyes. Had we not both of us been plunged into the deep waters of the past that are for ever flowing towards an ocean without marge and without bottom?

From Maria I went to the cottage of Mrs. Duffet, another old woman. She required no prompting. She remembered Mr. Powys. Had not her mother come to the very house in which she now lived so as to be nearer to the rectory? A duty had been required of her—the duty, namely, of twice a day suckling my father. Here, then, I was talking to my father's foster sister—this old woman and my father had been held up to the same fountain, had drunk from the same life-giving well. This was the daughter of the woman who had put wormwood to her dugs, sitting in the sun under Stalbridge Cross!

How would it be possible to catch, to hold for a moment, the quality of those magical hours of June sunshine, of June moonlight, down in that Dorset village? At night I wandered along Drew Lane far into the vale. On all sides of me recumbent cattle dreamed away their animal existence under hedges festooned with dog-roses already in bud. Barn-door owls with unfilmed eyes called to each other out of the hollow bodies of listening trees. One by one the lights of the village above the valley were put out. The old men dreamed, the old women dreamed, the boys and girls dreamed, and a grace, the solace of antiquity, sustained in Christian peace these ancient meadows.

The next morning I was waked by the treading of cows being driven through the street. All was once more astir. Above each little back garden, with its produce so neatly set out in rows, innumerable larks trilled. I left my hostess early and made my way in the direction of the next village. Often had I heard my father speak of a certain halter-path which led to Sturminster Newton, and I now had a mind to follow it. More like a lane than a path it turned out to be. Sturdy oaks flourished on each side of it. Presently I realised that I was overtaking a bowed figure, who, with a stick in her hand was picking her way across the ruts. I spoke to her. She had lived in Stalbridge all her life, she said. When she heard who I was she laughed aloud. She remembered my uncle Littleton well. "He used to run races along be I. He used to give I star cakes; they star cakes were as big round as a frying-pan and had currants in 'em." And then as the old woman gathered her memories about her, it was as though in that ancient mind time became discounted. The bracken that was uncurling on upright stems in the ditches belonged to the year 1927, but to the old cottage woman it opened upon a world where death itself was forgotten. "Tell him, tell him," she cried with excitement, "that ye met Nancy Curtis in the halter-path, the girl what used to run races for they star cakes—that will bring I back to the mind o'en."

I asked for her blessing and hurried on. How could I explain that she had given me a message to a soldier who had been lying dead in the dry soil of India already for half a century?